# KILLING IDOLS FOR

## REVIVAL: LIFTING UP JESUS CHRIST AND CHOPPING OFF HEADS

### OF 9 PRINCIPALITIES AND STRONGHOLDS IN CHRISTIAN MUSIC INDUSTRY AND IN MINISTRY TO CREATE CHRIST-FOCUSED REVIVAL AND A MOVEMENT OF HARVEST LABOR IN AMERICA

A BEHIND THE SCENES LOOK AT 9 ENEMIES OF GOD'S HARVEST

Esosa and Shereena Osai

ISBN-13: 978-0615594002 (WizdomHouse Publishing)

ISBN-10: 061559400X

## What People Are Saying About This Book

The book is raw yet loving... not an easy combo to pull off! - Loan Officer, Troy, MI

This book is actually helping me, it is really eye opening. - Pastor, Atlanta, GA

After the third read, I definitely felt more compelled to make sure I am not fornicating with the world, more open to God's way of doing things, and working on my prayer life to be spiritually aware of what is happening out here and cry out. - Real Estate Manager, Ann Arbor, MI

When I read this book I really felt the purity of the Lord pouring out. It felt like rivers of water were pouring not only with the testimony and message but with the Word to back it up... it changed me and how I saw things. What I love about the book is the transparency and the openness; it gave me hope for some challenges I was facing. It was exactly what I needed, an on time rhema word concerning some recent business dealings that I have been involved in. - Marketing Manager, Arcata, CA

Reading the book... it's kind of entertaining, it's pretty sweet. But the scripture references are very interesting. What's funny is - now I'm noticing that I am in a similar types of situations. Now I know how to handle these situations better and totally rely on God. I think it's good, a dope concept. It captures the entertainment side, and it gives the Scripture teaching points too. - Music Producer, Detroit, MI

A few things that are touched on are things I've battled, weighed and made decisions on in my own life. Some examples of those things are deciding what willI choose to let in entertainment-wise and frustration with double standard lifestyles/ secular imitation of Christian-labeled artists, among other things. I'm in a season of maturing, development and shaping and I'm enjoying it. - MBA Student, Chicago, IL

I think you've identified the main spirits that will attack revival and harvest in the Church: spiritual seduction and control. Those who have a call to be used to purify the worship in the church, Jezebel will always come at them to destroy the pure worship she sees. The control and seduction have as their end-goal the tearing down of true worship and the erecting of the false. This is Jezebel's specialty; she attacks true worship so that it becomes false. The chapters on Jezebel were outstanding! - Pastor, Dearborn, MI

The book moved me. It is written is such a way that it presents such a measure of vulnerability and exposure, but with humility. The stories help me to connect to the authors and the book because it depicts "real life". But the book doesn't just stop at the "good story" level — it adds a depth and richness of the Word searched out, illuminating the path to truth... - Educator, Ann Arbor, MI

Kudos... you have a heart for the Lord and a determination to reach others for Christ! - Gospel Music Radio Announcer, Detroit, MI

I like the book a lot! It has a powerful message—it's a deep message and a hard message, but a necessary message. The book leads me to want to examine my own life and identify areas where the enemy is scheming against my life or ways that my own indiscretions have become footholds. – Teacher, Detroit, MI

The images in the book give you something to identify with, and remember in your mind when you come across it. How the dreams and imagery of the characters come together was very nice... you have a pretty solid foundation to work with. It was kind of artistically stimulating for me. - Graphic Artist, Detroit, MI

This book is really unique how you tell the dream, and then you explain the dream by the circumstances. I've never even seen anybody do it like this... One thing I'm getting from it is its helping me to be even more careful with how I progress my ministry... It also kind of leads you on the path of teaching you how to interpret dreams. In my ministry, I'm trying to teach people that this is what God said would happen in the last days (dreams and visions). So many of my members that have been asking about that type of thing will be very interested in this book. First of all, what's good about this book is that it gives solid teaching, it's not fluff. People are tired of the shallow messages about 7 points for your best life, and they are hungry for more of the deeper things of God... Mainly because you can't have your real best life without going deeper in God. Second, its hitting a major need, a need that is almost unmet in the Body of Christ, and that's how to deal with their dreams and visions. - Pastor, Atlanta, Georgia

**When you finish reading, go to www.killingidols.com and leave your feedback, bad or good! Thanks!**

# DEDICATION

This book is dedicated to our grandparents and parents. We love you. You have paved a way for our generation to make a difference, and provided a great example.

This book is also dedicated to my two sons, Champion Luke and Arrow Joseph, whose births coincided with the inspiration behind the 1st and 2nd versions of this book.

# CONTENTS

## Matthew 10

26 **Fear them not** therefore: for there is *nothing covered , that shall not be revealed*; and hid, that shall not be known. 27 **What I tell you in darkness, that speak ye in light: and what ye hear in the ear, that preach ye upon the housetops.** 28 And **fear not them which kill the body**, but are not able to kill the soul: but rather *fear him which is able to destroy both soul and body in hell.*

1 Samuel 17

51 Therefore **David ran** , and **stood upon** the Philistine, and **took his sword**, and drew it out of the sheath thereof, and <u>**slew him, and cut off his head**</u> therewith. And when the Philistines saw their champion was dead , they fled .

Ephesians 6

12 For **we wrestle NOT against flesh and blood**, but *against* *principalities*, *against* *powers*, *against* the *rulers of the darkness* *of this world*, *against* *spiritual* *wickedness* in high places.

# PREFACE

# DREAMS: A SEAL OF INSTRUCTION

Part of our journey was learning how to hear God's voice through dreams. In the past I haven't paid much attention to my dreams. My interactions with dreams were very few and far between. I have a couple of dream interpretation books to help me out... but it was never a part of my consistent communication with God. Then I got married!

My wife is a dreamer, and she comes from a very prophetically gifted family. We had many dreams the first few years of our marriage, and we did not understand most of them. Many of them were scary to her so I tried to comfort her, pray for her, plead the blood of Jesus over our bedroom, rebuke demons, etc...

Then some of the dreams started to get more obvious and show up in our lives, and we figured out that maybe the dreams were warnings from God. Even though I didn't dream much, I was good at interpreting them. But some of these dreams were so weird, it wasn't until a few years later when we received a key of knowledge and were really were able to interpret all of them. That's when we decided to write this book, and we are using the insight God gave us in everything we do!

God spoke to many men through dreams (Joseph, Paul, Joseph, Daniel, etc...)

> *Job 33:14 For **God speaketh** once, yea twice, yet man perceiveth it not. 15 **In a dream,** in a vision of the night, when deep sleep falleth upon men, in slumberings upon the bed; 16 Then he **openeth the ears of men,** and sealeth their instruction, 17 That he may withdraw man from his purpose, and **hide pride***

> *from man.* 18 *He keepeth back his soul from the pit,*
> *and his life from perishing by the sword.*

God speaks to us several times. He'll give you a thought, then He'll remind you of a scripture. Then somebody will say something deep to you; you know it's from God. Then after all that, sometimes a dream can be that final seal on God's instructions for your life. He does this to people when they are slumbering in deep sleep. He opens their ears when they aren't distracted and busy with everything else. Your brain is active when you dream.

A seal can be a stamp of the King's Authority. Record your dreams, pray to interpret them, and **confirm them with scripture** to put God's seal on His instructions for your life. God definitely speaks to you, so believe Him to hear His voice while you sleep. We encourage you to write your dreams down whenever you have the opportunity to remember them.

I still don't remember my dreams as much as my wife does, but sometimes I do, and it helps. Let me give you an example:

One day recently the Lord reminded me of the scripture in Galatians 6 – "If anyone be overtaken in a fault, Ye who are spiritual, restore such a one in a spirit of meekness, lest ye also be tempted." I took note of it in my heart. Later that week I preached a message exposing one of the principalities described in this book. That same night I had a dream:

*I got a call that my brother (my real life blood brother) had been arrested for something. I came to get him and see the situation. The situation was pandemonium. People were rioting and throwing basketballs through the windows of houses, and burning things. On my way driving down Outer Drive, past 7 mile, I ended up driving too fast past a policeman in the left lane that was facing me. I swerved to the right, but I got stopped and got a ticket. Then somehow I ended up on the roof of the rioters, throwing basketballs through windows. Then I ended up in jail with my brother, confused. I was wondering what was going on, and asking around. There was a woman in the prison who worked in the entertainment industry who understood and was going to tell me.*

When I woke up and pondered the dream, I realized it was related to the exact same scripture that I had just been meditating on for a week. On my way to get my brother who had been overtaken in a fault, I got caught speeding and ended up in the same situation. The fear of the Lord gripped me, and it drove me to dig deeper into the scripture and meditate more deeply about the specific meaning of the word meekness.

The testimony in this book lets you into a few parts of our journey of learning how to interpret these dreams and use them to kill the enemies of God's dream – all while restoring our brethren with meekness.

## God's Instructions for this Book

Everything in this book is true. The dreams were dreamed, the testimony was lived, and the scriptures are true. This is our real life. Some of the dreams came before the events, as warnings. Some came after, to clarify what happened or to give insight. Most of the dreams we didn't understand until events unfolded.

Even though this was a time of tremendous difficulty, we know that **love never fails** (1 Corinthians 13:8). This account was not written to expose any person who may have been used to do wrong. There are many much more specific dreams and situations we could have shared in this book, but the full history of what was said and done is kept vague for a purpose. Love does not calculate evil (1 Corinthians 13:5).

We realize that there are times when we all "do not know what spirit we are of" (Luke 9:55). One of our favorite prayers is Christ's intercession of the Cross – "**Father forgive them, for they know not what they do**" (Matthew). We have forgiven all, and reconciled, and attempted to reconcile with the people involved. We have worked and partnered with hundreds of different people over the years, so please do not try to guess who did what. The overall majority of the people we have worked with have been awesome and fruitful Kingdom partners.

**This book is supernatural.** We did not ask for any of these dreams, or any situations that came with them. I wish we were smart enough to come up with all these characters and images ourselves, and connect them with the future, but we aren't. If we were, we would have avoided the situations altogether. We actually thought the dreams were from the devil and prayed against them at first. Much of what was revealed to us were things we did NOT want to know or experience.  We believe that most of the characters in the dreams represent spirits, not people. If we have succeeded in telling our testimony out of forgiving hearts, then after the last chapter of this book you will feel purified with reverence for God.

This book was written to expose the devil only. We know that **what the devil meant for evil, God meant for good**. We wished we could just teach what we learned without sharing what happened in our lives. That would be much easier. We wrote it this way because we had to. God made it very clear to us that our only remaining option to overcome the accuser was by the Word of our testimony. After the Blood of Jesus, **our testimony and our life-sacrificing obedience are how we overcome the devil** (Revelations 12:11). Especially when we considered the scriptural lessons learned, the supernatural nature of the dreams, and the needs of the Body of Christ in this hour – we knew this was not just for us. It has to be shared with all who hunger for God to move unhindered in the earth.

The Body of Christ absolutely has to rise up and exercise authority over evil. The title of this book is not meant to incite physical violence, only **spiritual violence**. When we talk about "Chopping Off Heads" we speak of cutting to the root and the spiritual source for hindrances to the Kingdom of God. These are Satan, his lies, his powers, his principalities, and his demons. However, Jesus Christ has given the Church all authority over the enemy, and the power to bind and loose.

> *Matthew 18:18 Verily I say unto you, Whatsoever <u>ye</u> <u>shall bind on earth</u> **shall be bound in heaven**: and whatsoever <u>ye shall loose on earth</u> **shall be loosed in heaven.** 19 Again I say unto you, That if two of you*

> *shall agree on earth as touching any thing that they shall ask , it shall be done for them of my Father which is in heaven. 20 For where two or three are gathered together in my name, there am I in the midst of them.*

When we get to the root of things, we will find that the source of all of the problems in the church and in the nations lies in the **churches' own toleration of idols, lies or wickedness on the inside.**

We know that no one person has all the insight concerning these dreams, or the full message that God was trying to get across. If you have any scriptural insight on interpreting any of these dreams, or confronting these issues that hinder the Body of Christ, please put a comment on the website for this book – www.killingidols.com!

It is our hope and prayer that by what God has shown us, people will be instructed into a higher level of wisdom in Christ. We hope that God's messengers and musicians will be purified and emboldened to hold fast to the **only spiritual Head which will not be cut off, which is Christ** (Colossians 2:17-19). We hope that this will be the generation that **seeks His face** (Psalms 24), to usher in the final harvest labor movement that will **fill the earth with knowledge of the Glory of the Lord. Come Lord Jesus!**

# BACKGROUND

This is by no means a full biography; it's just a summary outline of victories and attacks in our ministry. I wrote this testimony because after many years I noticed a pattern... Satan attacks in special ways to **hinder the Word from being fully preached**, and to stop God's people from **becoming a house of prayer**.

We don't wrestle with flesh and blood, but with principalities and powers. No person has the ability to orchestrate the trials that make our faith stronger – so we don't blame people. We are THANKFUL for Gods Salvation and Blessing, The Body of Christ's Support through the years, and for all the trials that have made us 100X stronger!

Jesus is KING. When the enemy attacks, we just hit him back... much harder. We do this by promoting Jesus as KING. God crushes Satan as we move forward with the gospel of peace on our feet.

> *Romans 16:20 And the **God of peace shall bruise Satan under <u>your feet</u>** shortly . The grace of our Lord Jesus Christ be with you. Amen*
>
> *Ephesians 6:15 And **<u>your feet</u> shod with** the preparation of **the gospel of peace**...*

Jesus loves us with a completely overwhelming passion and love. This passion fills us and gives us faith... it makes us believe. Since believe, we work our faith in ministry, by serving God and serving God's people, and reaching unbelievers with truth and love.

Satan hates our ministry with a passion... Because it unifies people around Christ, it doesn't include most religious traditions, it emphasizes the Word and the Spirit, and it reaches young people. Satan hates the Word of God being spread in a non-traditional way. Last, but probably most - Satan hates unified Prayer combined with music. Music and God's presence was his specialty before he was kicked out of heaven (Ezekiel 28:14-18). Helping to facilitate night & day prayer combined with music is one of the major end-goals of our ministry.

## How it all Started

### 1997

JESUS rescues my mind. Although I grew up in a Christian home, in my high school years I was enticed by the lure of sinful music, specifically the lyricism of some of the hip hop artists of the day. When I graduated from High School, the Holy Spirit started to deliver me and I decided I was going to live the faith and defend the faith in college. I didn't want to be one of the countless kids who grew up in church, then went away to college, got turned out by sin, and lost faith in God. So in the summer before I went to Michigan State University, I started reading the Bible and praying daily. I also went to Summit Ministries in Colorado, a camp to learn about the lies of secular education, so that I could defend my faith against professors preaching evolution and secular humanism.

On my second day at MSU, during my daily bible reading, I came across the scripture in 2 Corinthians 7:1, which says to cleanse ourselves from all filthiness of flesh and spirit. This scripture gave me a biblical motive to give up secular hip-hop. My mind had worked so hard to justify it over the years... but my heart was starting to change. Finally, I had a scriptural justification and command to give up secular hip hop music!

When you give up something for the Lord, He rewards you in this life and in the life after. Not long after I gave up listening to secular music I discovered some new Christian hip-hop and Rhythm and Praise artists. Then I brought my first 5 Christian CDs: Cross Movement, Boogie Monsters, Fred Hammond, VIRTUE, and Blood Brotherz. I was blown away by the quality of the music and the message in those gospel hip hop, gospel, gospel r&p, and gospel reggae albums. Soon God gave me a vision to be a gospel dj – to evangelize and spread His Word with music.

My life was heavily impacted by the Word of God. Then through a friend from high school, I become involved in a brand new campus ministry, Glory Phi God campus ministries. Since it was active, prayer filled, and on a college campus, it was much more than just going to church. That's when we became addicted to the lifestyle of a believer: doing bible studies, fellowshipping, having prayer meetings, preaching the gospel to win the campus to Christ. Somehow I came across Acts 2:42, and God showed me that this was the real Christian life.

> Acts 2:42 And they continued steadfastly in the **apostles' doctrine and fellowship,** and in **breaking of bread, and in prayers.**

## 1999

Eventually we started praying daily as a campus ministry at 6am every morning, as well as weekly on Friday nights. I was already falling in love with unified prayer. On a trip home from school, my mother gave me a set of teaching tapes from Mike Bickle on the Tabernacle of David concept in the bible. As I learned more and more about the house of prayer through the bible teachings and actually living a life of individual and corporate prayer, I fell even deeper in love with God.

I hear God's call for me and I decide to promote the Word of God through music, events, concerts, and eventually have a Christian Café that is also a house of prayer. I start djing for campus ministry and my friend's ministries.

## 2000

In college I realized for first time that sometimes different churches had different names because their denominations didn't agree with each other. I was really hurt by that. I came across someone teaching Psalms 133 in a book, and that planted unity in my heart. I also discovered 1 John 1:7, and that solidified it even more. Unity was my passion. In my Senior year at MSU, this all culminated in God leading me to start a ministry to unify all the campus ministries at MSU – called MSU Christian Alliance.

## 2001

I graduate from college, and feel called to go back to Detroit. I start working a job as an engineer while continuing to dj and serve in church and in other ministries.

## 2002

I refuse to go back to the normal "Church is for Sunday" lifestyle. I wanted the Christianity similar to Acts 2 that I experienced in college. I begin the promotion, evangelism, lifestyle ministry (bible studies, fellowships, outreach, Christian music, events) all while serving in my local church and working a full time job.

We started doing lots of events through friendship productions. We were building unity, saving souls, spreading the good word and good music. Growth. Unity. Music. We exist to create friends of God, that do whatever He commands them (John 14), and who hate sin and the worlds twisted ways (James 4:4).

## 2004

We get our first consistent café/event spot, and start doing bi-weekly events. I also live in a house with 3 other Christian brothers and we do bible studies and prayer meetings, and fellowships weekly.

## 2005

We promoted our first major concert. Within months I lost my job.

We are still promoting Christ through events, we hit back very hard within a few months.

## 2006

We planned our first prayer party. We call it ihop (I'm a House of Prayer), harp & bowl prayer events. We also planned a huge evangelism blitz at a major secular concert festival. As well as a free party.

Within weeks, all my equipment was stolen. I slipped and left my car cd player and my equipment in my van. Thieves got a bonanza of over $15,000 worth of dj equipment and gospel cds.

The Body of Christ supported, some of it was restored. Praise God. We hit back hard. We still did the prayer party, the evangelism, and a free party too at our club. We did another successful promotion with a gospel rap artist at the end of that year.

## 2007

I plan to get married. Soon after God reveals that it is time for marriage, I discover my wife, and I am amazed. She is spiritually custom-designed, she fits the God inspired vision that I had written in 2001. She is a perfectly complementary helpmate, and God brought her right to me. We plan to get married in 2008.

In our ministry we are persevering, and still promoting Christ.

## 2008

This is the winter where 5 straight major events were hit with snowstorms. 5 straight. It started in November 2007. The weather would be clean and clear for weeks, but when we had a major event there would be a snowstorm warning and several inches. The snow storms greatly impacted the number in attendance at the events. 5 straight events! It was ridiculous.

That spring we still had several good events, a couple of major promotions.

I got married to my wife. God is good. We try to glorify God through the promotion of our wedding, and with the ceremony. We threw a free concert as a wedding after party. It was a free concert with two worship bands, and we invited the whole city. It was a blast.

We had a huge successful promotion of the gospel with an awesome gospel rap artist. We are still hitting back hard.

Within 18 months of our marriage, we lost 3 vehicles to transmission problems. One of them had been given to us after we lost the first one. After losing the 3rd vehicle, we realized that maybe the transmissions in the vehicles were too weak to haul my sound equipment.

I remembered hearing that in dreams, cars represent ministries... so I guess we were being attacked naturally and spiritually.

Speaking of dreams... around that time is also when the dreams got really weird. They began speaking loudly, but we couldn't hear what they were saying. In the following chapters, dreams that my wife had will be recounted and the real life events that came with these dreams will be relived.

# 1

## JEZEBEL 1.0: IF YOU DON'T KILL HER, SHE'LL KILL YOU

**Enemy Profile:** Jezebel Seduces Kings into Spiritual and Natural Fornication. This spirit Uses Physical, Spiritual, Business and Political Power.

**Shereena's Dream**

**Jezebels: Summer 2008 – Spring 2009**

*We are in our bed together, cuddled, in love, in the depth of sleep. Sometime during the night I start dreaming...I dreamed that a woman dressed in red lingerie was on a lounge bed trying to seduce my husband. I cry out loud, Esosa wakes me, asking what's wrong. The dream is so real, and the emotions I feel are so real, I cry, and he holds me. He keeps asking me what is wrong. I am reluctant to reveal the dream to him. I do not want my new husband to feel that I doubt his love, but I am so saddened at the thought of it. For the first two and a half years of our marriage I dream continually about Esosa being seduced by other women or in bed with other women. In some dreams I knew the women, in other dreams they were strangers to me. But after every dream the pain was the same when I woke up. Esosa's love was so strong, as was his commitment to me. But the continual dreams of adultery perplexed and disturbed me.*

## Real Life

I was really annoyed with these dreams that kept waking up my new wife. She would be crying, tears rolling down her face. Sometimes the dreams made her so sad it was hard for her to talk and tell me what happened. I kept thinking that she thought I wanted to cheat on her. I didn't. I fight every man's battle, but I learned how to fight lust as a single man trying to be holy. Control your eyes by looking down at the path of your feet, and control your thoughts with words. I'm not a perfect man, but I love the Word of God. I also love my wife. I cherish her and don't want to do anything to hurt her or the marriage God has ordained.

I thought the dreams were from satan. I thought that he was trying to plant fear in my wife's heart. We prayed against the dreams, and pleaded the blood of Jesus over our bedroom and house, but they continued.

Soon after I was married I was blessed with a 2 - year contract for a new part-time job. It was perfect for me because I could continue to build up the ministry, and provide for my new family.

My desire at that time was to eventually be able to focus full time on promoting the Word through my events and other avenues. According to 2 Corinthians 9, those that preach the gospel should live off the gospel. We have a right to make money and provide for our families while doing what God has called us to do. The concert scene I set up was a way for my ministry to be funded and eventually build a Christian café and house of prayer where people could worship God day and night at all times with live musicians, as well as fellowship.

Meanwhile, the concerts were growing in attendance and influence. They went from averaging a couple hundred to several hundred people, and even went over one thousand in attendance.

## Why Promotion?

Even though we are doing concerts and events, our primary focus is to promote the Word of God. It's not about the artists or messengers more than it is about Christ the Head. Even more ultimately, everything we do is about promoting God's Word, because God exalts His Word above His Name.

> *Colossians 2: 18 Let no man beguile you of your reward in a voluntary humility **and worshipping of angels [messengers]**, intruding into those things which he hath not seen, vainly puffed up by his fleshly mind, 19 **And not** holding the Head, from which all the body by joints and bands having nourishment ministered, and knit together, increaseth with the increase of God.*

> *Psalms 138:2 I will worship toward thy holy temple, and praise thy name for thy lovingkindness and for thy truth: for **thou hast magnified thy word above all thy name.***

---

**Magnify**: Hebrew (Gadal)
To grow, become great or important, promote, make powerful, praise, magnify, do great things

---

We use promotions as a tool to promote the Word. We don't just try to get people in the door, we are preaching the gospel in the streets and in the media as we promote. We are seeking to preach a scriptural message through the media. We see souls saved and ministered to in the streets and in the media. For us, the event is only the confirmation of the message. The musical artist is not a messenger that we worship, the musical artist brings confirmation of the message that we have worked hard to promote in the culture.

We have found that spreading the Word through music, media, and lifestyle can have a major impact on people's souls.

We have sought to find creative ways to promote the Word of God, and the name of Christ, not just the musical messengers. We care more about being faithful to the message than getting everyone to like us. So we have done it all, from teaching apologetics, exposing the lies of Islam, Jehovah's Witnesses, Atheism, confronting compromise, false doctrine, sinful movies, sinful music, so-called Christian entertainment (church based movies that contain more foolish talk, cross-dressing and adultery than truth), lies in politics (philosophies that come from satan, spread in churches through politics) etc... We have spoken on all these issues, through our promotions, events, and communication networks built in our ministry.

So, in the course of promoting the Word, sometimes I end up confronting hindrances to the Word - usually secular entertainment, false religion, and a spirit of compromise.

As a wise Christian rap artist once told me, you have to play offense AND defense in the Kingdom of God, not just offense. We lift up Christ, and we expose the enemy. We promote the Truth, and we tear down lies. Of course, as I do this, it creates controversy at times. People like to argue, and sometimes I lost people's support and friendship for the stands I took. But through it all I kept doing what I was called to do. I matured and grew, learned how to declare the truth in love, and tried to cut off arguments before they started. I kept pressing on, and really didn't take seriously the demons that were trying to discourage me through people.

After one particularly large promotion and concert we threw, literally overnight I went from dealing with small demons to dealing with principalities. The crowd was big, the money was big, and I knew things were changing for the better; but I did not know that Jezebel was coming for my head. Keep in mind, this whole time my wife is continually having dreams about me sleeping with what she called Jezebels, at the time we think those dreams are about physical adultery. Let's look at the first instance of Jezebel in the Bible.

## Scripture

### Who is Jezebel?

> *1 Kings 16:31 And it came to pass, as if it had been a light thing for him to walk in the sins of Jeroboam the son of Nebat, that <u>he took to wife Jezebel the daughter of Ethbaal king of the Zidonians, and went and served Baal, and worshipped him.</u>*

> *1 Kings 21:25 But there was none like unto Ahab, which did sell himself to work wickedness in the sight of the LORD, <u>**whom Jezebel his wife stirred up**</u> . 26 And he did very abominably in following idols, according to all things as did the Amorites, whom the LORD cast out before the children of Israel.*

Jezebel was a queen in Israel. Israel was the nation that God chose to re-introduce His Truth back into the earth through the Messiah, Jesus Christ. So Israel was meant to be a Godly nation, but it became defiled by its own sin. Ahab was one of the kings of Israel, and he was wicked. Jezebel got into Israel by marrying a wicked king. She was from a foreign nation, and she brought her foreign gods with her into Israel. The main false god was called Baal. Jezebel stirred her husband up to worship this false god.

Baal was the god of rain. People trusted this idol to "make it rain." In an agricultural society, rain represented good crops, and therefore wealth. Baal was always paired with Asherah, a god of fertility. Their idol worship literally consisted of priests performing sexual rituals.

In plain terms: **idolizing Baal & Asherah** back then is similar to **idolizing power, money & sex** today.

A couple of possible reasons for Ahab and Jezebel's marriage were of course, politics and money. Political marriages like this were common in those times. Kings married foreign wives to gain **influence** and to be better able to do **business** with other nations. Unfortunately, marrying foreign wives often brought false religion into the nation of Israel.

## What did Jezebel do?

> *1 Kings 18:13 Was it not told my lord what I did when* <u>**Jezebel slew the prophets of the LORD**</u>, *how I hid an hundred men of the LORD'S prophets by fifty in a cave, and fed them with bread and water?*

Jezebel killed prophets of the true God. That was part of her agenda, because she worshipped gods that represented wealth, power, and sex (Baal & Asherah).

## Who is Elijah, and what did Elijah do?

> *1 Kings 16: 1 And Elijah the Tishbite, who was of the inhabitants of Gilead, said unto Ahab, As the LORD God of Israel liveth, before whom I stand ,* <u>**there shall not be dew nor rain these years,**</u> <u>but according to my word.</u>

> *1 Kings 18:37* <u>Hear me, O LORD, hear me, that this people may know that thou art the LORD God, and that</u> <u>**thou hast turned their heart back again.**</u> *38 Then the fire of the LORD fell, and consumed the burnt sacrifice, and the wood, and the stones, and the dust, and licked up the water that was in the trench. 39 And* <u>when all the people saw it, they fell on their faces: and they said , The LORD, he is the God; the LORD, he is the God.</u> *40 And Elijah said unto them,* <u>Take the prophets of Baal;</u> *let not one of them escape. And they took them:* <u>**and Elijah brought**</u> <u>**them down to the brook Kishon, and slew them**</u>

> *there*. *41 And Elijah said unto Ahab, Get thee up , eat*
> *and drink ; for there is a sound of abundance of rain.*

Elijah is a messenger of God. One of the first things you see Elijah do is confront the false god Baal by exercising the **authority of God over the rain**. Then, after some time, after the nation's **economy is crushed by famine because there is no rain...** Elijah sets up a confrontation between the prophets of Baal and himself. God answers by fire, and the prophets of Baal look foolish. Then he kills all the prophets of Baal. He does this in hope of turning the hearts of the nation back to God.

**How does Jezebel respond?**

> *1 Kings 19:1 And Ahab told Jezebel all that Elijah had*
> *done, and withal how he had slain all the prophets*
> *with the sword. 2 Then **Jezebel sent a messenger***
> ***unto Elijah,** saying, So let the gods do to me, and*
> *more also, if I make not thy life as the life of one of*
> *them by tomorrow about this time.*

Everything Elijah did was a direct confrontation of everything that Jezebel stood for. Instead of repenting, Jezebel turns her heart harder, and threatens to kill Elijah. Unfortunately, instead of chopping her head off too, Elijah runs away. God had to anoint another prophet (Elisha) and king (Jehu) to finally destroy Ahab and Jezebel.

The spirit of Jezebel showed up in the New Testament too. Wherever there is Elijah, there is Jezebel.

Before Jesus Christ came, John the Baptist showed up in the spirit and power of Elijah, preaching repentance and specific practical ways to turn away from sin and back to God.

> *Matthew 11:11 Verily I say unto you, Among them*
> *that are born of women there hath not risen a*

> *greater than John the Baptist: notwithstanding he that is least in the kingdom of heaven is greater than he. 12 And from the days of John the Baptist until now __the kingdom of heaven suffereth violence , and the violent take it by force__ . 13 For all the prophets and the law prophesied until John. 14 And if ye will receive it, __this is Elias (Elijah),__ which was for to come.*

In the course of his preaching, John the Baptist ended up speaking against what king Herod and Queen Herodias had done, for their sinful relationship. Herodias hated John the Baptist so much, she ended up working out an evil plan. Herodias had her daughter dance for Herod. Then Herod, excited by the sensual dance, promised he would reward her with whatever she wanted. Her mother Herodias told her to tell him exactly what she wanted: John the Baptists' head on a platter.

So John the Baptist was beheaded.

> *Mark 6:18 For John had said unto Herod, It is not lawful for thee to have thy brother's wife. 19 Therefore Herodias had a quarrel against him, and would have killed him; but she could not: 20 For Herod feared John, knowing that he was a just man and an holy, and observed him; and when he heard him, he did many things, and heard him gladly. 21 And when a convenient day was come, that Herod on his birthday made a supper to his lords , high captains, and chief estates of Galilee; 22 And when __the daughter of the said Herodias came in, and danced, and pleased Herod__ and them that sat with him, the king said unto the damsel, Ask of me whatsoever thou wilt, and I will give it thee. 23 And he sware unto her, Whatsoever thou shalt ask of me, I will give it thee, unto the half of my kingdom. 24 And __she went forth, and said unto her mother, What__*

*shall I ask? And she said, The head of John the*
*Baptist. 25 And she came in straightway with haste*
*unto the king, and asked, saying, I will that thou give*
*me by and by in a charger the head of John the*
*Baptist. 26 And the king was exceeding sorry; yet for*
*his oath's sake, and for their sakes which sat with*
*him, he would not reject her. 27 And immediately the*
*king sent an executioner, and commanded his head*
*to be brought: and he went and beheaded him in the*
*prison, 28 And brought his head in a charger, and*
*gave it to the damsel: and the damsel gave it to her*
*mother.*

## Interpretation

Today's prophets of money and power do not dress in robes and burn animals on altars. To prophesy means "to declare." The prophets of today declare their beliefs using speeches, music, movies and entertainment. To entertain means to "hold in the mind." Wicked entertainers and liars work hard to deceive. They make products and productions so that you can hold their lies in your mind. As you hold their images, thoughts, and words in your mind, they permeate your soul. You begin to follow lies and idols instead of truth.

Just as the prophets of Baal are still around, Jezebel is still around. Jezebel is a spiritual seductress in authority. She represents false authority among the people of God. She represents spiritual adultery, the worship of power, money and sex among God's people. Jezebel hates God's prophets. If she cannot seduce them, she seeks to kill them and destroy them in any way possible.

There is a Jezebellic spirit of compromise seducing the church, and it has affected many people in the church. During this time period when Shereena was having these dreams, and even up until now, many people were falling away due to the inroads made by movies, music, and politics that posed as good but were sourced in evil. Jezebel, as a spirit of compromise, was trying to seduce me in more ways than I knew at the time... She couldn't quite fully do that, because I held to the Word of Christ, and risked my reputation and finances to declare the word of God, and expose the enemy. When I started to expose her biggest prophets of money and sex (the top secular rappers and singers of today), she changed her strategy from seducing me to killing my voice.

## Application

**Jezebel is a Spirit of Seduction for spiritual, financial, and then physical fornication.**

Be pure from lust: physical, financial, and spiritual.

**Men: Look down to protect your eyes.** Gaze upon your path, and look where you are going, naturally and spiritually. Use your mouth to control your thoughts. Declare your love for God and (if you are married) your love for your wife vocally. Words control thoughts.

**Women: Dress modestly, and teach younger women** to dress modestly. You should not dress to show off your breasts, or your butt, or your shape.

**Declare God's truth at the risk of your own reputation and finances. If you don't, you will end up in spiritual idolatry.** Don't be a friend of the world, be an enemy of the world (James 4:4). You don't have to be mean, but you do have to speak the truth in love.

If you don't kill Jezebel, she will kill you. **Playing nice with a spiritual adulterer will always backfire.** If you see lies, call them out. When God's people see from His perspective - and care more about His thoughts than our reputation, influence, and success – then we will see God do a huge work in our land.

Don't be a wicked weak Ahab, and let Jezebel in the kingdom for political convenience, financial success, or influence.

**Be an Elijah.** Turn people's hearts away from idols and back to God.

Support ministries that are bold and confront the idols of this world. Let the chips fall where they may, let people place themselves where they want to be in relation to the truth. When the truth is exalted, people will show you who they really are.

Lust: Chop its Head Off!

Being Nice to Idols: Kill it!

Choosing Influence and Money over Obedience: Kill it!

**As we purify our hearts and turn to God and away from physical, spiritual, and financial idolatry, God will give us clear prophetic insight and a clear voice to call a nation to repentance, and we will see His fire fall and His rain fall!**

**2**

# THE JUDAS KISS – EVERY MINISTRY MUST PREPARE

**Enemy Profile:** Judas betrays the true purpose of God by doing what he thinks instead of what God wants. God gets what He wants anyway, but Judas suffers woe.

**Shereena's Dream**

*Henry Ford Dream: October 2009*

*I dreamed that a large, older Caucasian man that looked like he was from the 1930s was in our house. He was dressed in a vintage three piece navy blue suit, with a pocket watch chain looped out of his vest pocket. In my dream I remember thinking the man was like Henry Ford. He was trying to take authority and control in our house. He was setting up his factory operation in our home. He brought many workers with him who were carrying out his orders in every room of the house. The operation was very efficient, quick and orderly. At first he was diplomatic about it and tried to negotiate with us. Then he tried to take full control. He was trying to boss Esosa, and he had demon spirits working for him like mechanics and engineers all over the house. As he gained more control in the house he let down his façade and his speech got sloppy. He started speaking like an old mob boss. He had his operation going all over the house. And the demons that were working for him were very small like dwarfs. One of them rolled out from under our bed as if he was working on a car, and looked up at me, and I saw that he had no eyes. While the man was in the house my husband went to the front door to the mail slot to check the mail. He picked up the mail and was looking through it, the man came and snatched our mail from Esosa and said "Give me that boy!"*

## Real Life

After one particularly large promotion I came across a series of youtube videos exposing some of the satanic influences behind major rap and r&b artists. The videos exposed the true pagan and idol worship behind some of the top secular songs of the day. It was also revealed that a goal of these artists and the industry behind them is to lead the masses in idol and satanic worship.

Of course, I promoted these videos to my facebook friends, email list, and blog... It was a very hot message at the time. And since one of my goals is to expose lies and promote truth, I blasted these videos through every avenue. The videos were extremely popular; they were viral before I even saw them. People talked about them all over the place, even at the school I worked at.

The secular music expose' that was being promoted created a lot of controversy. Many people's eyes were opened, and even unbelievers became more discriminating with their musical choices. I remember hearing kids that weren't even saved say "I don't listen to them anymore; they worship satan." However, many people did not like that it was being exposed.

One of my supporters had begun to confront me continually about what I was doing to expose the devil. He kept telling me that my ministry brand was being ruined. He had talked to many people about me, and said many people stopped liking me because of the videos and my expressed opposition to sinful music. He said people didn't want to support me or my ministry because of what I was posting related to some particular secular music artists. He wanted me to stop what I was doing. He felt that the videos I was posting were too extreme. He expressed that people truly liked and connected with the secular artists that were discussed in the videos. By me posting and promoting the videos, I was upsetting and isolating people from myself which in turn might damage the "brand" of our lifestyle ministry. Even though we had just hosted the biggest concert we'd ever had, He said that concert attendance wasn't yet big enough because people were too offended with the message I promoted.

This man had supported our ministry for a few years, and had been a supportive brother. I had listened to him in the past, and he gave good advice, so I tried to hear him out. I made my preaching more balanced and gentle, but I didn't stop it. For me, the preaching is the point, not concerts. The concerts are to extend the influence of the preaching. He still wouldn't give up, and kept coming to me trying to convince me to stop. Finally, after weeks of back & forth, he gave me some "options." I could stop preaching. Or I could keep preaching, and give up all the "big concerts" to another brand that he would create. But if I didn't stop, he was going to stop supporting me, and work to replace my ministry with a new brand. I could do all the little events, and they could do the big events.  That way he could make more money, and therefore reach more people.

I would not bend any further away from the Word of God, so my supporter left to form a replacement brand.

### Scripture

Jesus said that the servant is not greater than his master. So if one out of twelve of His disciples was a Judas - a betrayer – then we can be warned of a similar possibility in our ministries.

However, in some ministries, the ratio can even be as high as one out of three. Jesus said that in the last days, many shall be offended, and shall betray one another (Matthew 24). He also said there would be many false prophets that shall deceive many. With false prophets such as Lady Gaga openly declaring the advancement of the Judas spirit with songs about Judas, how do we overcome the spirit of Judas?

### Recognizing the Judas Anointing - Why did Judas do what he did?

Judas was earthly minded. He was called "Iscariot." That means he was a part of a group of people who were Zealots and carried a dagger.

"Siccari" means "dagger men." Zealots were motivated by sociological, economic, and political factors. They believed that the Messiah would come, take over, and rescue Israel from Roman rule with earthly power and financial force.

Some of Jesus' disciples were Zealots, or influenced by the ideas of the Zealots. These disciples were the ones that took the most offense when Jesus told them that he would die, or when they saw Christ doing money-wasting activities.

Judas in particular is never recorded calling Jesus Lord, or professed life sacrificing obedience. He is only recorded as calling Jesus "Rabbi," which means teacher. This could mean he only saw Jesus for His earthly usefulness. He was earthly minded.

Judas Iscariot was a Zealot, and he was in charge of the money for Jesus' ministry.

> *John 13:29 For some of them thought, because <u>Judas</u>*
> *<u>had the bag,</u> that Jesus had said unto him, Buy those*
> *things that we have need of against the feast; or,*
> *that he should give something to the poor.*

Judas complained about the sacrificial worship of Mary to Jesus. Judas was motivated by money, and masked it with pragmatism and a false desire to give to the poor. His true desire was to steal and get money and power for himself.

> *John 12:3 Then took Mary a pound of ointment of*
> *spikenard, very costly, and anointed the feet of Jesus,*
> *and wiped his feet with her hair: and the house was*
> *filled with the odour of the ointment. 4 Then saith*
> *one of his disciples<u>, Judas Iscariot,</u> Simon's son, which*
> *should betray him, 5 Why was not this ointment sold*
> *for three hundred pence, and given to the poor? 6*
> ***This he said, not that he cared for the poor; but***

*__because he was a thief__, and had the bag, and bare what was put therein.*

Jesus rebuked Judas for murmuring against the worshipper. Mark 14 shows that when Judas saw the money wasted on worship was when he first decided to find a convenient way to betray Jesus.

*Mark 14:3 And being in Bethany in the house of Simon the leper, as he sat at meat, there came a woman having an alabaster box of ointment of spikenard very precious; and she brake the box, and poured it on his head. 4 And there were some that had indignation within themselves, and said, Why was this waste of the ointment made? 5 For it might have been sold for more than three hundred pence, and have been given to the poor. And they murmured against her. 6 And Jesus said, Let her alone; why trouble ye her? she hath wrought a good work on me. 7 For ye have the poor with you always, and whensoever ye will ye may do them good: but me ye have not always. 8 She hath done what she could: she is come aforehand to anoint my body to the burying. 9 Verily I say unto you, Wheresoever this gospel shall be preached throughout the whole world, this also that she hath done shall be spoken of for a memorial of her. 10 __And Judas Iscariot, one of the twelve, went unto the chief priests, to betray him unto them.__ 11 And when they heard it, they were glad, and promised to give him money. __And he sought how he might conveniently betray him.__*

## Pragmatism

Pragmatism in a spiritual sense is choosing your own thoughts over God's thoughts.

**prag·ma·tism:**
1. character or conduct that emphasizes practicality.
2. a philosophical movement or system having various forms, but generally stressing practical consequences as constituting the essential criterion in determining meaning, truth, or value.

Pragmatism is a philosophy that severely overdoes practical thinking - to the point of betraying God and doing what we think will work. Judas's pragmatism was the driving force of his betrayal of Christ. He wanted to get his will done his way. He wanted **control**. God got His will done, anyway. Judas ended up being instrumental in God's will, but on the wrong side. "Woe to him by whom He is betrayed."

> *Luke 22:22 And truly the Son of man goeth , as it was determined : but* **woe unto that man by whom he is betrayed!**

**Practical <u>obedience</u>** to the will of God (no matter what the cost or the loss), is the way of the cross, and the way of Christ. Practicality taken to the extreme seeks to avoid the way of suffering in favor what is considered pragmatic according to human thought.

After Jesus was arrested, beaten, and about to be crucified, and Judas saw the damage he had done, he changed his mind when he saw Jesus was condemned. So that means one of two things:

A. Judas didn't think Jesus was going to be condemned. Judas was using his mind to work his own plan, so that Jesus could go ahead and take over on earth instead of dying on the cross. Or

B. Judas betrayed Jesus out of offense and repented later. He figured out that Jesus was innocent after he made the mistake of betraying him.

In either case, it's clear that Judas did not believe in **God's way of sacrifice**, choosing to try and **get his agenda completed in worldly ways**. He didn't agree with the ways of God.

> *Matthew 27:3 Then Judas, which had betrayed him,* <u>*when he saw that he was condemned, repented himself*</u> *, and brought again the thirty pieces of silver to the chief priests and elders, 4 Saying,* <u>*I have sinned in that I have betrayed the innocent blood*</u>*. And they said, What is that to us? see thou to that. 5 And he cast down the pieces of silver in the temple, and departed, and went and hanged himself.*

## What Types of Ministries Attract Judas?

Any ministry under the headship of Christ will attract a spirit of Judas. Music ministries especially attract the spirit of Judas. Why? Because Judas gives Satan direct access to the anointing of Christ, so that he can corrupt His followers.

Satan was a musician. God created him with instruments inside of him. He was in charge of the presence of God. Just as Judas had access to Jesus through being one of the twelve disciples, Satan had access to God's throne (the mountain of God), because he was in charge of "covering" it with an atmosphere of musical worship.

> *Ezekiel 28:12 Thus saith the Lord GOD; Thou sealest up the sum, full of wisdom, and perfect in beauty. 13 Thou hast been in Eden the garden of God; every precious stone was thy covering, the sardius, topaz, and the diamond, the beryl, the onyx, and the jasper, the sapphire, the emerald, and the carbuncle, and gold<u>: **the workmanship of thy tabrets and of thy pipes was prepared in thee**</u> in the day that thou wast created. 14 **Thou art the anointed cherub that covereth** ; and I have set thee so<u>: **thou wast upon the**</u>*

*__holy mountain of God;__ thou hast walked up and down in the midst of the stones of fire. 15 Thou wast perfect in thy ways from the day that thou wast created, till iniquity was found in thee. 16 By the multitude of thy merchandise they have filled the midst of thee with violence, and thou hast sinned: therefore I will cast thee as profane out of the mountain of God: and I will destroy thee, O covering cherub, from the midst of the stones of fire. 17 Thine heart was lifted up because of thy beauty, thou hast corrupted thy wisdom by reason of thy brightness: I will cast thee to the ground.*

We all know what Satan did. He betrayed God and took 1/3rd of the angels with him (Revelation 12:4). He wanted God's worship for himself.

Well just like Satan was annoyed with Jesus being worshipped, Judas was annoyed with Jesus being worshipped. Just like Satan wanted to steal the glory, Judas wanted to steal the money. The Bible says that Satan entered into Judas. Satan entered into Judas to get Satan's will done.

*Luke 22:3 Then entered Satan into Judas surnamed Iscariot, being of the number of the twelve. 4 And he went his way, and communed with the chief priests and captains, how he might betray him unto them. 5 And they were glad, and covenanted to give him money. 6 And he promised, and sought opportunity to betray him unto them in the absence of the multitude.*

## How did Jesus deal with Judas?

Jesus always called out **Satan** when he saw **earthly-mindedness** in His disciples, whether it was Judas, Peter, or any of them.

*Matthew 16:21 From that time forth began Jesus to shew unto his disciples, how that he must go unto Jerusalem, and suffer many things of the elders and chief priests and scribes, and be killed , and be raised again the third day. 22 Then Peter took him, and began to rebuke him, saying, Be it far from thee, Lord: this shall not be unto thee. 23 But he turned, and said unto Peter, <u>Get thee behind me, Satan</u>: thou art an offence unto me: for <u>thou savourest</u> not the <u>things</u> that be of God, but those <u>that be of men</u>.*

*John 6:70 Jesus answered them, Have not I chosen you twelve, and <u>one of you is a devil?</u>*

Jesus knew that earthly mindedness led to betrayal, and told his disciples.

*John 13:21 When Jesus had thus said, he was troubled in spirit, and testified, and said, Verily, verily, I say unto you, that <u>one of you shall betray me</u>.*

*Matthew 26:34 Jesus said unto him, Verily I say unto thee, That this night, before the cock crow, thou shalt deny me thrice (Peter).*

Jesus still befriended his earthly minded disciples. He called Judas friend while he was betraying him with a kiss. He also reconciled with Peter after Peter denied him.

*Matthew 26:50 And Jesus said unto him, **<u>Friend</u>**, wherefore art thou come? Then came they, and laid hands on Jesus, and took him.*

*John 21 [After Jesus had raised from the dead] 17 He saith unto him the third time, <u>Simon, son of Jonas,</u>*

*lovest thou me? Peter was grieved because he said unto him the third time, Lovest thou me? And he said unto him, Lord, thou knowest all things; thou knowest that I love thee. Jesus saith unto him, Feed my sheep.*

## How does prosperity relate to the Judas Anointing?

**Prosperity God's way** : Abraham – Obedience, Sacrifice, Suffering, Faith, Giving, Blessing, for Distribution to God's people

**Prosperity Satan's way** : Judas – Scheme, Manipulate, Steal, Disobey, Avoid Suffering, Betray God's Purpose with a Kiss, for selfish earthly uses

Judas and the Pharisees paired up to kill Jesus. Judas was a thief, and the Pharisees were envious and covetous. Jesus looked at the hearts of the Pharisees. He saw that everything they did was for results in the eyes of man, and it was an abomination to God.

*Luke 16:13 No servant can serve two masters: for either he will hate the one, and love the other; or else he will hold to the one, and despise the other. Ye cannot serve God and mammon. 14 And the Pharisees also, who were covetous, heard all these things: and they derided him. 15 And he said unto them, Ye are they which justify yourselves before men; but God knoweth your hearts: for that which is highly esteemed among men is abomination in the sight of God.*

God doesn't see like man sees. In stark contrast, God actually despises the things that men look up too. What is highly esteemed and respected in the eyes of men (big money, big power without obedience) is actually **an abomination** to God.

In contrast, Judas, (the Betrayer) was one who despised the extreme giving of worship. He masked it by saying it was for the poor, but really it was because he was a thief with a wicked heart. He was all about the money, he wanted to see it all and manage it. He also never submitted Himself to the extreme sacrifice of the Cross. He was wrapped up in His own intelligence and ability, and ended up betraying the true purpose of God

Be careful of your views on how to obtain God's prosperity - or success in God's purpose and plan for your life. Your views of success and how to obtain it should always line up with scripture and NEVER be motivated by pride, money, or worldly strategies. Even when pursuing God's plan, it must be done God's way. If you do it your own way or in earthly-minded ways, **you give Satan access to your mind**.

> *Jeremiah 9:23 Thus saith the LORD, Let not the wise man glory in his wisdom, neither let the mighty man glory in his might, let not the rich man glory in his riches: 24 But let him that glorieth glory in this, that he understandeth and knoweth me, that I am the LORD which exercise lovingkindness, judgment, and righteousness, in the earth: for in these things I delight , saith the LORD.*

## Judas's Woe

Judas ended up committing suicide. When we take the nature of Judas, we end up committing suicide spiritually. Judas's woe is not always literal suicide – it's killing yourself spiritually, destroying your eternal reward, and sealing your eternal fate. Some disciples will get to heaven and find out that all of their work was burned – it was worthless wood, hay and stubble instead of gold, silver and precious stones (1 Corinthians 3:12). Some disciples won't even make it in. They will say how many works and preaching they did for Jesus, but Jesus will reject them because they didn't do the Father's will, and they chose to work iniquity instead (Matthew 7:22-23).

## Interpretation

When my wife told me about that dream (with the man like Henry Ford) I knew exactly what it was. It was one of the few dreams that I could interpret immediately, because being from Detroit and having worked in the auto industry in the past, I understood what the industrial spirit was all about. Henry Ford was known for being a very pragmatic, self-made man. That philosophy is very pervasive in our region.

The Bible says that those that are earthly minded are enemies of the cross (Philippians 2). Practical thinking can be a good thing, if used properly. Practicality, and "doing what works" is okay, as long as it doesn't trump obedience to God. Pragmatism is a man-made philosophy of thought. The wisdom of God surpasses the wisdom of man by far.

The proverbial "road to hell" is paved with good intentions. This dream showed the spiritual nature of what was happening in our ministry. Principalities were influencing people with good intentions, and according to the dream they were set on taking what was ours because they thought they could do better by keeping it politically correct. Industrial pragmatism and pride were the tools they were using to justify their actions.

## Application

**The Judas Anointing is pragmatism over obedience, which ends up betraying the true purposes of God.**

Always choose obedience to the Word of God over excellence.

Always choose obedience to the Spirit of God over convenience.

Always choose obedience to God over results.

Always choose obedience to God over what works in the eyes of man.

**Use practical wisdom and intelligence to obey God,** not to usurp obedience to God.

Take up your cross and follow Jesus Christ all the way. Arm your mind to suffer for righteousness, and don't avoid it.

Don't put making a profit or having results in man's eyes before declaring and standing for the truth of God that hurts.

Intellectual Pride: Chop it Off!

Pride in Riches: Kill it!

**As we move beyond our own earthly minded ideas and inventions, and follow what God wants to do in our cities, we will see God's Power flow to cause real repentance and a bigger Soul Harvest than we can ever imagine!**

# 3

# FIGHTING DEAD MEN'S BONES

**Enemy Profile:** Dead Men's Bones have been dead for a long time, but they still hold control over what can be said and done by living people.

**Enemy Profile:** Hypocrites are actors in real life, who view ministry as a performance before people, not before God.

**Shereena's Dream**

*Skeletons with Swords: October 2009*

*I dreamed that Esosa and I were fighting skeletons with swords inside of them, behind their rib cages. I managed to get a small sword out of one of the skeletons. Esosa was trying to get his big sword out of another skeleton, but he could not kill it. Esosa was down on the ground. I tried to give him the little sword I had in order to kill the skeleton that he was fighting to get the big sword, but Esosa did not want to use the sword I had because he thought it was too small.*

**Real Life**

Around this time I was trying to promote another concert. This concert was supposed to feature two artists in particular that were from different ends of the theological spectrum.

To me, that was an awesome opportunity. I still believe heavily in Unity in the Body of Christ, and I was very excited about promoting that show, and especially preaching the message leading up to the show. I thought that it was going to be spiritually powerful, and it had never really been done this way before.

Although this seemed like a great concert tour to get involved with and promote I should not have done it. My wife had strong reservations about it, but all I could see was the ministry opportunity and the momentum. We had just done the biggest concert in our ministry's history. The cost of doing the tour was not outrageous. We weren't going to make a lot of money, but it would more than break even and be a great promotion of unity. We had the momentum of the success of the last concert that would propel us.

Unfortunately, a few weeks after we booked it, that's when the supporter turned against our ministry philosophically and financially. Our money was already tied up. It was too late to cancel the concert for a refund, so we had to push on.

About a month after that, we found out that one of the main artists booked on the tour had been caught living in the sin of adultery, and could not conduct ministry so he would not be in the tour line-up.

We tried to change the artists in the concert line-up and push on, but things kept getting worse, as more wickedness in the character of those in the industry was being revealed.

### Scripture

> *Matthew 23:27 Woe unto you, scribes and Pharisees,* ***hypocrites****! for ye are like unto whited sepulchres, which indeed* ***appear beautiful outward****, but are* ***within full of dead men's bones****, and of all uncleanness.*

Jesus said that some of the people in charge of religion in His day were hypocrites, and like clean tombs full of dead men's bones within.

## Dead Men's Bones

The hypocrites that Jesus said had dead men's bones were people that followed traditions over the word of God.

> *Mark 7:13 **Making the word of God of none effect***
> ***through your tradition**, which ye have delivered: and*
> *many such like things do ye.*

They also overdid their honor of righteous prophets of the past, and at the same time they sought to kill the prophets of today.

> *Matthew 23:29 Woe unto you, scribes and Pharisees,*
> *hypocrites! Because **ye build the tombs of the***
> ***prophets, and garnish the sepulchres of the***
> ***righteous,** 30 And say , If we had been in the days of*
> *our fathers, we would not have been partakers with*
> *them in the blood of the prophets. 31 Wherefore ye*
> *be witnesses unto yourselves, that **ye are the***
> ***children of them which killed the prophets**.*

The Pharisees thought that they were righteous because they gave so much honor to the prophets of the past. But spiritually, they were prophet-killers, because they sought to kill the new message that God was bringing in their generation. In their zeal to protect and honor the old they destroyed their own legacy.

> *Acts 7:51 Ye stiffnecked and uncircumcised in heart*
> *and ears, **ye do always resist the Holy Ghost**: as your*
> *fathers did, so do ye. 52 Which of the prophets have*
> *not your fathers persecuted? And they have slain*
> *them which shewed before of the coming of the Just*
> *One; of whom ye have been now the betrayers and*
> *murderers:*

Most of the harsh rebukes of Jesus and the Apostles were against those who were resisting the Holy Ghost. We need an understanding of the Word of God as opposed to the habits, customs, and traditions of men, and what we think works. We also need an awareness of what the Holy Spirit is doing in every generation, especially the current one.

This is not really about whose ministry is the most correct... this is about the children, and the next generation.

Jesus Christ is in charge of His Church. He is the Head. The Holy Spirit is in charge of releasing fresh revelation of the Word in every generation. He reveals all truth (John 15). God's mercy endures, His truth to all generations (Psalms 117).

> *Matthew 9:17* <u>*Neither do men put new wine into old*</u> <u>*bottles:*</u> *else the bottles break , and the wine runneth out , and the bottles perish: but* <u>*they put new wine*</u> <u>*into new bottles,*</u> **and both are preserved**.

New wine needs new wineskins. There are new movements, and therefore new organizations and organisms that God needs to build every generation. The new will not fit inside the old. But the new needs to honor the old, and the old needs to allow the new to operate, so that both are preserved.

But unfortunately, in the history of the Church, new wineskins, new organizations, and new things that God is doing are attacked. Also, the new generation attacks the old.

As I have been planning for my family, God has shown me that I need to pass on to my family more than what I know, and the doctrine I know. I need to pass on a hunger for God's Spirit and what He is always currently doing. I don't want my grandchildren worshipping my dead bones, or the dead bones of the founder of any church, denomination, or movement; because if they do so, they will end up spiritually dead and deaf to what God is doing in their generation.

We need an understanding of the Word and an Awareness of what the Holy Spirit did and is doing in every generation. A true spiritual legacy is humility and a hunger for the Word and Spirit of God. My children won't survive on my revelation. They may die if that's all they get, because the times will have already changed.

> *Isaiah 59:21 As for me, this is <u>my covenant</u> with them, saith the LORD; **My spirit** <u>that is upon thee, and **my words** which I have put in thy mouth,</u> shall not depart out of <u>thy mouth, nor out of the mouth of thy seed, nor out of the mouth of thy seed's seed,</u> saith the LORD, from henceforth and for ever.*

Believe God for the Word and Spirit to fall on each generation. God will always do new things. The hearts of the fathers must turn to the children, and the hearts of the children must turn to the fathers (Malachi 4).

Now Let's talk about Hypocrisy:

## On Adultery and Hypocrisy in Christian Artists and Leaders

As long as the Church of the Lord Jesus Christ has been in existence, there have been false converts, weak brethren, false apostles, as well as honest believers that make mistakes. We all have been sinners at one time, and we still fight against sin.

There are plenty of pastors with children by different women in "their" congregation, and plenty of Christian artists that don't live what they sing.

Even King David himself slept with his neighbor's wife Bathsheeba, and then killed her husband. However, God had mercy on Him, because David confessed and forsook his sin. Even then, David reaped exactly what he sowed. His own daughter was raped by his own son, then one of his sons killed the other. Then the son that killed his brother tried to kill David and take over the kingdom! Plus the baby he had with Bathsheeba died. David had a brutal family life because of what he allowed into his family (2nd Samuel).

God is merciful and he will forgive you personally. David was still considered righteous, and a man after God's own heart, because of his repentant heart and faith in God's mercy. But you will still reap what you sow! That's an Immutable Spiritual Law.

*Galatians 6:7: Be not deceived; God is not mocked: for **whatsoever a man soweth, that shall he also reap**. 8: For he that soweth to his flesh shall of the flesh reap corruption; but he that soweth to the Spirit shall of the Spirit reap life everlasting.*

## Spiritual Law #2 – Confession and Exposure

Another scriptural promise that we should all be aware of is this: Whatever is done in secret will be seen in the light...

*Luke 12:1 Beware ye of <u>the leaven of the Pharisees, which **is hypocrisy.**</u> 2: For <u>there is nothing covered, that shall not **be revealed**</u>; neither hid, that shall not be known. 3: Therefore <u>whatsoever ye have spoken in darkness **shall be heard in the light**</u>; and that <u>which ye have spoken in the ear in closets **shall be proclaimed**</u> upon the housetops.*

You CANNOT HIDE ANYTHING! It's a spiritual principle! All sin is the result of believing a lie. One of the biggest and simplest lies Satan tells you is that you are powerful enough to keep sin a secret. It's IMPOSSIBLE. The longer you delay confession the worse it gets for you.

This is why you must confess your sins. The bible says whoso hides their sins will not prosper or be successful at it or anything else. But whoso confesses and forsakes shall have MERCY.

*Proverbs 28:13: He that covereth his sins shall not prosper: but **whoso confesseth and forsaketh them shall have mercy.***

This is why I personally try to catch and kill my sins in the thought stage, before they turn into words and actions. I know that God isn't just on the outside of me, He's inside of me looking at the video screen playing in my mind! If I notice myself lusting, or even cursing or saying non-blessings in my head, I'll confess it to God while it's still in my head. Otherwise, I know that I will reap what I sow, and I will not be able to hide it. It will be shouted from the rooftops and airwaves. Another benefit of doing this is that it builds intimacy, closeness and openness with God.

## Ministry and Music

Do we throw away the Psalms because David sinned? No. Even the chapters before Psalms 51 are still scripture.

Do we throw away Proverbs because Solomon didn't obey them? No.

It's the same thing with Christian lyrics... If it's Word-based, then it's anointed by God. The Word of God is anointed. It's our job to obey it and live it and promote it.

However, there are influences that we need to be aware of that will cause even the most scriptural lyricist to become a hypocrite, or an actor just performing lines. We will talk about that later on in this book.

Non-Christians LOVE to see bold saints fall into sin, and they love to call them hypocrites, because they think it gives them an excuse not to love or believe in God at all.

BUT when judgment day comes, everyone will stand before God and be judged by God, and their own conscience will give witness that they are wicked without Christ's mercy. There will be no excuses except the grace and mercy of Christ.

Hypocrites and actors in the churched will get judged too. If they don't obey Him, Jesus will declare that He never knew them. We all should fear God, tremble at His Word, and ask God for mercy. But judgment only **begins** in the house of God (1 Peter); it doesn't end there!

When non-Christians see believers being exposed, they should not be haughty. They should actually fear God, and be careful to repent, because that means judgment is coming even harder and quicker for them! God always purifies HIS people first before the ungodly get theirs.

> *1 Peter 4:17 For the time is come that judgment must begin at the house of God: and if it first begin at us, what shall the end be of them that obey not the gospel of God? 18: And if the righteous scarcely be saved, where shall the ungodly and the sinner appear?*

**Hypocrite:**
1. one who answers, an interpreter
2. an actor, stage player
3. a dissembler, pretender, hypocrite

A hypocrite is simply a person who is not true. They are actors in real life. Remember that Jesus said in Luke 12:1, the doctrine of the Pharisees was hypocrisy. They were actors and professional pretenders. They were pretending in real life! Jesus promised that if you are a pretender, the truth will definitely come out. It's a spiritual law.

So here is the option: you will either confess the sins, or it will be shouted from the housetops. Either way, there is nothing hidden. Exposure is inevitable! There is no need to gossip or spread rumors, because eventually, it will be heard in the light!

## Judgmental?

Some people like to say that if you preach the Truth, you are being judgmental, and somehow that causes you to be a hypocrite. Please read this scripture aloud:

> *1 Corinthians 7:9 Know ye not that the unrighteous shall not inherit the kingdom of God? Be not deceived: neither fornicators, nor idolaters, nor adulterers, nor effeminate, nor abusers of themselves with mankind, 10: Nor thieves, nor covetous, nor drunkards, nor revilers, nor extortioners, shall inherit the kingdom of God. 11: And such were some of you: but ye are washed, but ye are sanctified, but ye are justified in the name of the Lord Jesus, and by the Spirit of our God.*

Well, is reading that scripture aloud judgmental? The issue is not whether we can speak the Truth or not; the issue is: are we living the Truth, or being actors in real life?

This world is corrupt, our sin nature is real, and the devil is on the attack. But our Faith is the Victory that overcomes the World! In the Blood of Jesus, Victory is guaranteed.

## Interpretation

Dead Men's Bones are the traditions of dead men making the Word void of its true power. The skeletons had the swords in them, but the skeletons were obviously dead. The swords represented the Word of God. Jesus related dead men's bones to hypocrisy. Religious hypocrites are like dead men's bones. They have the Word but their dead traditions make it void of its power, which was shown by the swords being held within the skeletons.

When the teachings of men are elevated as equal with the bible, it is very easy to fall into the trap of men's traditions, and keep one void of the real power of God. One becomes so concerned with keeping a certain doctrine of a dead man that they begin to think that God can only move according to their understanding or teaching of the doctrine. They hang on to a few parts of scripture that pertains to the doctrine, instead of holding to the full counsel of God's word.

I believe that me trying to get the big swords out of the skeletons may have represented me attempting to partner in preaching with artists that were hypocrites at the time. I believe that what I was trying to do was right according to the Word (getting the big sword) and using it, but I wasn't being sensitive to the Spirit (represented by my wife's sword). The Holy Spirit is our Helpmeet as we seek to glorify the Word (Jesus). God uses dreams, visions, and guidance from the Holy Spirit to instruct us.

I wish I had known about this dream at the time, I didn't even find out about it until I told my wife that we were going to write this book, a couple years later. But I probably would not have understood it then anyway.

## Application

Don't assume that people are living the Word they are preaching. Verify. Know them that labor among you.

**Seek the power that lies within the Word of God, but don't neglect the Holy Spirit.**

Be sensitive to God, and **know no man after the flesh**, or their outward characteristics. (2 Corinthians 5:16)

**No one is perfect - but have a standard** of who you partner with, even if they are Christians.

**Don't overestimate anyone's spiritual maturity.** Lay hands suddenly on no man, neither be partaker of other men's sins: keep thyself pure (1 Timothy 5:22). Be very careful of the ministries that you promote.

Avoid Pride in Real Practical Ways: Sin gets in under pride... Don't put artists and popular ministers on a pedestal, when they should be equal (not just theologically, but practically). Keep a true Kingdom lifestyle of humility, fellowship, and brotherhood. Make yourself equal to the "lowest" brother you know in a practical way.

Don't Be Contentious: One practical evidence of pride is contention (Proverbs 13:10). A minister or artist is beefing with someone, or in strife, and that's how Satan gets in. Satan also gets into marriages by pride, then contention. If you feel like you are in a contentious fight with someone, humble yourself and let them win. Speak the truth and your belief and move on.

Travel with Your Wife or Team: We need to do the simple things like travel with our wives. Peter and the other apostles who were married (1 Corinthians 9:5) did this. If you don't have a wife, bring your teammate. The New Testament is full of lists of Paul's teammates; most of them were NOT his peons, slaves, or armor-bearers... most were his co-laborers, co-apostles, and brothers. Jesus didn't even start His ministry until he had a team. Ministry is TEAMwork!

**Fast Weekly**: Some people don't really obey Christ Jesus's command to fast that much. If you are heavy in ministry you need to be heavy in fasting. Even if you're not doing a lot of preaching you should be fasting regularly as a part of the kingdom lifestyle as a believer. (Matthew 6, Matthew 9:15). Fasting is brutal for your flesh, it helps keep you disciplined, and it just simply **multiplies the grace** on your life.

**Get Off the Stage:** If you are a Christian artist or minister, go house to house, not just stage to stage. Teach your sphere of influence to live the lifestyle of the Kingdom of God. Teach whatever scriptures you learn on a weekly basis. Do bible studies. Throw house parties. Host prayer meetings. People need brotherhood, house-to-house fellowship, and lifestyle discipleship, not just stage-to-stage-to-stage-to-stage ministry. Those days are officially over. Stage-to-stage ministry alone leaves people empty and immature as professional spectators. And by itself, it keeps Christian artists and ministers as actors on stage. When no one sees your real life it is easy to live one way on stage and another way by yourself.

**Keep it 50/50:** Match your ministry-to-others time with your ministry-to-the-Lord time. If you are hosting a 3-hour event, first minister to the Lord in your closet for 3 hours. You can call it "50/50 Ministry." This will keep you balanced.

Resist the urge to exalt dead men. Thank God for prophets, denomination founders, and movement initiators of the past. Honor leaders, fathers, and mothers, then seek God and press into God's Word for today.

**Study Church History for the purpose of understanding the context** of what the Holy Spirit is doing today, not to exalt dead men's bones. Study the Scriptures to find what God wants to say today!

**Don't ever resist the Holy Ghost!** Flow with what God is doing, instead of trying to make God flow with what man may have done in the past.

Being an Actor in Real Life: **Chop It Off!**

Traditions of Men that Make the Word of None Effect – **Chop Them Off!**

**As we move beyond dead men's bones into the passionate heartbeat of God for our generation, we will see a Union of the Word's Truth and the Spirit's Power. Our testimony will be real, and the world will know that Jesus is real because of our Oneness and love.**

# 4

# SHADE: A TIME OF TESTING

**Enemy Profile:** Persecutors — members of the world system will always persecute believers, but God uses persecution to test, try, and most importantly separate us from evil.

**Shereena's Dream**

*Shade: December 2009*

*Dreamed that a friend was standing outside on our porch and he pulled a shade down over our bedroom window. The time on the shade read 10:00pm in red, alarm clock digital numbers.*

## Real Life

This was definitely a time of testing. We had money invested in a concert with minimal support and not enough of a headlining artist. My supporter had already left in the middle of the promotion to form their own brand and carry out their new purpose to replace my ministry.

Then I found out main artist from the concert had fallen into sin and could not minister. We tried to get a refund. The organizer would not give refund, not even a partial refund. The organizer would not guarantee a sufficient replacement artist until several more thousands were paid (even though we already paid a significant deposit for the artist that could not minister). We could not promote the event, sell tickets, or get more money to pay the balance we still owed.

So if we cancel the concert, we lose everything. But we can't promote it, even though we've paid thousands, because the artists are not settled. Since we can't promote it, it's hard to sell tickets and get more money to get the new artist settled. Investors are forming a competing company, and have already said they will not support financially any more.

So now we're out of half the money: but we can't promote, we can't get refund, and we have minimal support. I feel like I'm between a rock, a hard place, and an abyss. I try to keep a good attitude, hustle up extra money somehow. I end up promoting it the best way I possibly can.

Last minute promotions worked okay, but not enough to replace the money we paid for the artists that didn't show up. We paid for plane tickets for artists that didn't show up. We paid deposits for artists that didn't show up. There was so much confusion, artists that were supposed to be at the concert sabotaged it by advertising that they wouldn't be at it. I tried to work things out with them, but the damage was done. The organizer admitted he owed us money but refused to pay.

The concert still glorified God heavily. The Word was glorified, and the artists that did show up rocked the house for Christ. Even when you mess up, the Word still works! However, we still had a huge financial loss that should never have been. The concert would have been easy to promote if we could have promoted the way we normally do.

Then, after the concert, when things should have been reconciled, they got worse and worse. We were promised a refund that never happened, and free plane tickets that never happened. The charge for the makeup concert kept going up and up until it didn't make sense to do. No one was in my corner to help me recover.

This was a very tough time for my family, a time of testing. We experienced abandonment, lies, sabotage, stealing, emotional pain, family strain, all in one period. I had a lot of sleepless nights, and ended up in debt for the first time in my entire ministry. There were so many unrelated factors that came together against us, I felt like I was caught in a whirlwind. I could not have imagined that all these things would have happened beforehand.

It was a tough period. I was patient for a long time, but towards the end I got angry a few times, and tried to sin not! I started to get sharp, because my trust of people was beginning to break down.

That experience didn't break us though. I still had a certain measure of joy, though it was not as much as I had before. But we kept our faith and worked on another tour. This tour was smaller, but it went pretty smoothly and was a lot of fun, and God was glorified even more.

## Scripture

*Hebrews 5:8 Though he were a Son, **yet learned he obedience by the things which he suffered;***

*1 Peter 4:12 Beloved, think it not strange concerning the fiery trial which is to try you, as though some strange thing happened unto you: 13 But rejoice, inasmuch as **ye are partakers of Christ's sufferings;** that, when his glory shall be revealed, ye may be glad also with exceeding joy.*

*Psalms 146:3 Put not your trust in princes, nor in the son of man, in whom there is no help.*

## The Value of Persecution

Homosexual marriage crusades, Government enforced infanticide, violent massacres, talk of one world government and currency to fix a created "crisis..." The daily news sounds like a prophecy from the bible! Are you ready for the times? Or are you just waiting to disappear?

Jesus said to watch and pray that you enter not into temptation. But do we really know the SPECIFIC temptation that he was talking about?

## Persecution is a form of the Mercy of God

Why is persecution a form of mercy? Because it separates you from those who are about to get judged by God. Let's take a look at some of the wicked systems that will be destroyed by God very soon.

## Babylon the Great Whore Gets Destroyed

> *Revelations 18:4 And I heard another voice from heaven, saying, Come out of her, my people, that ye be not partakers of her sins, and that ye receive not of her plagues.5: For her sins have reached unto heaven, and God hath remembered her iniquities.*
>
> *24: And in her was found the blood of prophets, and of saints, and of all that were slain upon the earth.*

In this scripture, God is telling his people to come out of the system of Babylon the Great Whore (a personification of the one-world economic and religious system) that is filled with sin. In this same chapter we see that she (Babylon) kills the saints. The love of money is the root of all evil (1 Timothy 6).

In Revelations 18 we also see that God is punishing this system with death and destruction. All the false religions that have persecuted and killed people all over the world including: extreme Islamists, Buddhists, Communists, false Christians, crooked businesses, and wicked governments, dictators, etc... will be destroyed.

Take a look at Revelations 18. In it you will see that the Babylon system controls commerce and economies, products of all types, governments, kings, businessmen, entertainment, music, slaves, and the souls of humans.

## Jesus is going to Kill Wicked Government Leaders!

Do you know that your Lord and Savior is going to literally kill thousands of people in the end of this time period? Some people will call me extreme for repeating what is in the Bible. We need to embrace the entire mission of our Savior in order to fully understand Him, and to help prevent people from falling into that judgment, the severity of God. Knowing the terror of the Lord motivates us to persuade men and speak the truth in love (2 Corinthians, Galatians 5).

> *Psalms 110:5 The Lord at thy right hand shall strike through kings in the day of his wrath. 6: He shall judge among the heathen, he shall <u>fill the places with the dead bodies</u>; he shall <u>wound the heads over many countries</u>.*

The Lord will kill many government authorities (kings, prime ministers, presidents, dictators). He will fill places with dead bodies, and wound the heads over many countries. This is literally going to happen.

> *Ezekiel 39:11 And it shall come to pass in that day, that I will give unto Gog a place there of graves in Israel, the valley of the passengers on the east of the sea: and it shall stop the noses of the passengers: and there shall they bury Gog and all his multitude: and they shall call it The valley of Hamon-gog. 12: And <u>seven months shall the house of Israel be burying of them</u>, that they may cleanse the land.*

This scripture in Ezekiel talks about a huge army from the North coming against Israel in the last days. Some say it will be the army of Russia and Iran. God will kill them all. God will kill so many people that they will have to hire people to bury them all, and it will take seven months to finish! This is a bible prophecy that has not happened yet. It will happen soon.

> *Revelations 19:17 And I saw an angel standing in the sun; and he cried with a loud voice, saying to all the fowls that fly in the midst of heaven, Come and*

> *gather yourselves together unto the supper of the great God; 18: That ye may <u>eat the flesh of kings, and the flesh of captains</u>, and the flesh of mighty men, and the flesh of horses, and of them that sit on them, and the flesh of all men, both free and bond, both small and great. 19: And I saw the beast, and the kings of the earth, and their armies, <u>gathered together to make war against him that sat on the horse</u>, and against his army.*

This scripture in Revelation describes the Battle of Armageddon. Lots of death will happen here. I'm sure you get the point by now. Let's move on to a poignant question:

## What if You Were a Part of the Wicked System?

What if you were a part of the Anti-Christ army that Jesus would eventually kill (upon His return)? What if you were drafted into an anti-Christ Army and they decided to go invade Jerusalem... or kill members of illegal house churches? Wouldn't that suck!? What if you were a wicked business person that was a part of the Babylon system, or a false religion that worshipped your tribal God's or idols? What if you rose to the top of religion, business, or government by doing things Babylon's way?

The mercy of the Lord Jesus dying for your sins can forgive you of those sins and make you a part of God's family. But there is another form of Gods mercy that separates Christians from participating in the sins of their nation and/or any system that they may be involved in. This mercy comes to all true believers who desire to live Godly. It's called PERSECUTION!

When the unbelievers persecute you, they SEPARATE you from their company, so you don't have to be judged by God along with them!

**Persecution is like being pushed off a train track!** Your response could be:

"Thanks, you should probably jump off too before that train comes!"

**Persecution is like being pushed out the door of a burning building!** Don't worry about your knee getting scraped. Your response could be:

"Thanks, but you should probably leave too!"

Persecution is actually a form of MERCY. Persecution prevents you from participating in systems that will soon be judged by God. It's God's practical way of separating you from the judgment of the world. Your persecutors also get a chance to repent, when they see that you are not fazed by their persecution. It also gets you a great reward.

> *Luke 6:22 Blessed are ye, when <u>men shall hate you</u>, and when they shall <u>separate you from their company</u>, and shall reproach you, and <u>cast out your name as evil</u>, for the Son of man's sake. 23: Rejoice ye in that day, and leap for joy: for, behold, your reward is great in heaven: for in the like manner did their fathers unto the prophets.*

This is one of the reasons Jesus said: "resist not evil." This is one of the hardest parts of the Kingdom of God, but if we understand what is going on spiritually, we can do it.

> *Matthew 5:39 But I say unto you, That ye <u>resist not evil</u>: but whosoever shall smite thee on thy right cheek, turn to him the other also. 40: And if any man will sue thee at the law, and take away thy coat, let him have thy cloak also.*

**Don't be Terrified!**

> *Philippians 1:28 And <u>in nothing terrified</u> by your adversaries: which is to them an evident token of perdition, but to you of salvation, and that of God.*

> *29: For <u>unto you it is given in the behalf of Christ</u>, not only to believe on him, but <u>also to suffer</u> for his sake;*

Don't be alarmed, or terrified by your enemies hating you or persecuting you for Christ's sake. If you are unshaken by their persecution, it will be an evident sign of their impending doom, and a sign of your heavenly help and intervention from God! It may give them a chance to change.

It's your **responsibility** to not only believe in Christ, but to suffer for his sake. Now that's something you don't hear a lot! Yet, it's all over the New Testament. If you believe and live according to the Word of God, you will suffer. Suffer what? You will suffer persecution and hatred from the devil and demonically inspired people. You will have victory in your God-given purpose, but you will have haters. It's a guarantee.

> *2 Timothy 3:12 Yea, and **<u>all that will live godly</u>** in Christ Jesus <u>shall suffer persecution</u>.*

But what I want you to understand about persecution is that it is actually a **BLESSING**. It's a **form of Mercy from God**, because it practically separates you from those who are doomed to judgment, and sets you up for a literal intervention of salvation from God.

Changing your mental understanding to embrace this particular type of suffering instead of avoiding it will make you a strong and fruitful Believer.

> *Acts 5:40 And to him they agreed: and when <u>they had called the apostles, and beaten them</u>, they commanded that they should not speak in the name of Jesus, and let them go. 41: And they departed from the presence of the council, <u>rejoicing that they were counted worthy to suffer shame</u> for his name.*

Why did the apostles rejoice that they were **beaten and abused** for the cause of Christ? Were they weird, or just really excited? No, they were just not as **SPIRITUALLY BLIND** as you and I sometimes are.

They had the spiritual eyesight to see the **VALUE** of what had just happened to them, and they were genuinely happy about it.

We cry when our Christian message doesn't sell as much as a wicked one. Then we compromise so we can reach more people. We cry when people talk bad about us. Apostles rejoiced when they were beaten and commanded by authorities not to speak in the name of Jesus.

Let's see how the disciples learned this new mindset.

### What's the Biggest Temptation?

Before Jesus was crucified He told the disciples to pray that they enter not into temptation. They didn't pray, so they all ended up entering into the temptation.

What was the temptation? The temptation that they entered into was **to avoid persecution by denying Jesus to be accepted by the world** (like Peter did), or **actually joining in the persecution of Jesus to be a friend of the world** (like Judas did).

Jesus told them to pray that they would resist entering **the temptation to avoid suffering**, which is persecution by a wicked system... which is a form of Gods Mercy to separate you from the judgment of that wicked system. The disciples did not pray, they slept, so they did not understand that concept, and they all ended up avoiding persecution and denying Jesus (entering into the temptation).

After the Resurrection, much day & night unified prayer, and the infilling of the Holy Ghost, they finally understood Jesus' Words and were changed from the inside.

Jesus **succeeded** in avoiding the temptation to avoid persecution, suffering, and death! Why? He prayed. When He prayed, He was very honest with the Father. He told God **three times** that He didn't desire the suffering, and He asked the Father to check out any other options to get the redemption of humans accomplished. But ultimately He submitted and did His Father's will.

> Luke 22...*Pray that ye enter not into temptation.*
> *41: And he was withdrawn from them about a*
> *stone's cast, and kneeled down, and prayed,*
> *42: Saying, Father, if thou be willing, remove this cup*
> *from me: nevertheless not my will, but thine, be*
> *done.*

## The Significance of Flesh Sacrifice

Jesus was beaten with a cat of nine tails (a whip with jagged metal and spikes of glass fastened to it) until blood came out of every part of his body.

His persecutors put a crown of long, thick, thorns on his head, so blood was pouring down His face too.

They stuck nails through His hands and feet, and hung him on a tree. He died from not being able to breath, because his lungs were crushed by the weight of his body, because he couldn't hold Himself up on the cross. His body lost too much blood, so He was weak.

At what point did He say, "It is finished?" It was at the point of His death. This was the point where He said "It is Finished."

We know that afterward, He took the keys of hell and death (Rev. 1), and that his soul was not left in hell (Psalms 16). We know that in 3 days, He rose from the dead with all power. Those things were very important to part of purposes of God, i.e, Jesus going into the spiritual realm and spoiling principalities and exercising authority, etc. But when did He say **it was finished**? It was finished at the cross. It was already finished **at the point of His death & suffering**.

What was finished? Our **redemption** was finished! This was the point where He purchased you and I to be His partners, and the Church to be His Bride. His death was the point where "**it**" **was finished. This was what He was looking forward to. The reason He died was accomplished right there at the point of His death.**

Jesus suffered to be able to purchase us. We were the joy that was set before Him (Hebrews 12).

Why is it important to know at what point "It is finished?"

When you know the **value**, or **reward** of suffering for what is right, you are no longer afraid to suffer. When you realize that suffering is actually a form of mercy that separates you from a wicked system and leads to a greater reward, you will avoid the temptation to escape your persecution and suffering for righteousness. Jesus knew the reward for suffering; therefore He prayed that He would avoid the temptation to bypass suffering. Since Jesus suffered in this way, we can expect the same thing. He warned us of this repeatedly.

Yes anyone can suffer, but **redeeming spiritual and supernatural power** is manifested when the innocent suffers for what is right. People like Gandhi, Martin Luther King, and Rosa Parks took this one principle and changed nations. What can we do with it? We can turn the world upside down for the true King Jesus (Acts 17:6)!

Don't suffer for your disobedience, sin, or foolishness. Suffer for what is right.

> *1 Peter 2:19 For this is thankworthy, if a man for conscience toward God endure grief, <u>suffering wrongfully</u>. 20: For what glory is it, if, when ye be buffeted for your faults, ye shall take it patiently? but if, when ye do well, and suffer for it, ye take it patiently, this is acceptable with God. 21: For even hereunto were ye called: because <u>Christ also suffered for us, leaving us an example, that ye should follow his steps</u>:*

**Follow Christ's Example and Suffer in Your Flesh; It Will Help You Out!**

> *1 Peter 4:1 Forasmuch then as Christ hath suffered for us in the flesh, arm yourselves likewise with the same mind: for <u>he that hath suffered in the flesh hath ceased from sin;</u> 2 That he no longer should live the*

> *rest of his time in the flesh to the lusts of men, but to the will of God.*

When you resist satisfying the lust of your eyes, that's a death to your flesh.

When you resist satisfying your lust and desires for illicit sexual pleasure or excess food – that is sacrificing yourself.

When someone persecutes you for Christ's sake, or because you are not sinning, that's a sacrifice that is well pleasing to God.

When you make less money by testifying of Jesus than you could make by not testifying and committing your work to Jesus, then you are blessed even more by God.

**Let's Learn to Embrace Our Suffering Instead of Avoiding It**. I'm NOT talking about suffering from sickness, or suffering because of your sin, or from the results of being lazy or disobedient and unwise. Biblically, the ONLY suffering that is a blessing is the suffering that comes from **righteous acts**. Let's pray that we don't enter into **temptation to avoid** this form of Mercy from God.

## Interpretation

My wife looked up what 10:00 represented in "Interpreting the Symbols and Types" by Kevin J. Conner, a book for interpreting biblical symbols. It said that the number ten represents a time of testing and trial.

> *Revelations 2:10 Do not fear any of those things which you are about to suffer. Indeed, the devil is about to throw some of you into prison, that you may be tested, and you will have tribulation **ten** days, Be **faithful until death**, and I will give you the crown of life.*

## Application

Be ready for your time of testing.

**Pray that you would never enter into the temptation to refuse God's Mercy and Blessing by avoiding persecution for your faith in God.**

**At God's throne in prayer, verbally commit to always testifying of Jesus when it's not popular.**

**Proclaim that persecution is an escape from a corrupt system that will soon be destroyed!**

**Proclaim that some of your greatest blessings from God come from when you are not accepted by man!**

**Never Avoid** speaking the truth of Jesus in order to avoid being hated on for doing so.

**Never Avoid** doing what God's Word says in order to avoid being left out, or talked about, or persecuted.

**Always Support** persecuted Christians that you see by praying for them, speaking out for them, and supporting them financially. Identify with them, being in the same Body as you. (Hebrews 12:3) This could mean supporting the Christian kid who gets talked about at school, praying for Chinese house churches, or giving to a ministry like Voice of the Martyrs.

**Always Remember** that persecution is a good thing. It's a Form of God's Mercy, and it's a Blessing with great rewards. Renew your mind on the issue of suffering.

In tough times, dig into the Word and Prayer even more. Sadness will drive you deeper into the enemies trap if you let it.

Realize that Persecution is a blessing, because it's actually God's way of separating you from the punishment that will come to those who do wrong, and put you on a higher level in the Kingdom of God.

Realize Gods ultimate purpose in everything is to make you like Jesus Christ. You haven't learned Christ until you've learned the ABCs of Love: Jesus loved friends that **A**bandoned Him, disciples that **B**etrayed Him, and haters that **C**rucified Him

**There will be hard times for God's people. But if we keep our faith, then after our time of testing, we will come out on top, as pure gold, redeeming many from sin just like Christ our example!**

# 5

## SNAKE AND HARLOT BUSINESS

**Enemy Profile:** Snake spirits represent Satan and demons - they are deceivers and devourers; small snakes bite & poison, big snakes wrap and squeeze.

**Enemy Profile**: The Harlot spirit represents the world system - it prostitutes God-given gifts for the enemy's use when it mixes with the world's ways in business.

**Shereena's Dream**

*Playing with a Demon: November 2010*

*My mom dreamed that Esosa was playing a game with a demon. The demon was presenting different investments for Esosa to invest in. He made the investments seem as if Esosa was investing in the Kingdom of God, but they were only traps to deplete money from our family. The demon was evil, and was sitting, taking our money. Esosa was playing the game, and he then had to pay the demon $3,000. Esosa handed me the money to go give to the demon. I was very upset and I knew that the investments and the game was a trap. But I was trying to follow and obey Esosa. My mom commanded the demon to stop taking our money and the evil spirit responded "Why? He's been playing with me." In the dream we had a sense of innocence and were truly trying to do work for God.*

## In Bed with Jezebel: November 2010

*Esosa and I were at a hotel or bed and breakfast. It was a large Victorian-style white house, with light colored furnishings. We only rented a room but we had access to the entire house. We had our things in drawers and rooms all over the house. There were other people staying in the house also. Esosa and I were in our rented room. The large king size bed took up most of the space in the room. There was a dresser with a mirror at the foot of the bed. There was also a small bathroom in our room. Esosa was sitting up on the bed resting his back against the headboard. He was holding his smart phone in his right hand reading something on it; he was very distracted from what was going on. Esosa was sitting on the right side of the bed. There were two female prostitutes in the room with us, one was African American and the other was Caucasian. They were in the bathroom getting dressed in lingerie and fixing their hair and make-up to get in bed with Esosa. He had already prepared for them and was sitting in bed waiting. The prostitutes were young with upbeat personalities. I was walking around talking and laughing with Esosa and the prostitutes, pretending I was ok with everything, but I was feeling disgusted. I did not know what to do. I knew what was happening was wrong, I wanted to leave but I did not want to leave my husband with the prostitutes. I did not want to participate, but I could not bear the thought of my husband being intimate with these whores. When the women came out of the bathroom, dressed in lingerie and ready to get in bed with my husband, I pretended like I was ok with it and went to the dresser to get my lingerie out so I could join in. I figured if I was there maybe I could try to keep control of the situation somehow. As I was sitting at the foot of the bed, going through my lingerie drawer I turned and looked around the room. My husband was still sitting up in the bed, distracted and reading on his phone, two prostitutes were standing on the left side of the bed waiting to get in bed with MY husband and here I was trying to find lingerie so I could join in with it all?! I became extremely angry and decided I could NOT allow this to happen. I stood up and went into a jealous rage! I started screaming "No, I am not going to allow this!" I started tearing the room apart, throwing things down, and throwing things out of drawers. I screamed at Esosa several times "If this is what you wanted why did you marry me?!" Then the women laid on the bed, Esosa pulled the African American woman up and asked her to go wash her hands. As I continued to rage and would not allow the act to go forward, the prostitutes realized they were not going to be able to do what they came for which meant they would not get paid either. They had plans on taking half of our money. I told them had they gone through with it they would have only gotten a portion of half. But once they realized they were not getting anything they got mad and went into the living/dining area of the house and started breaking our things. We had very expensive crystal, china and expensive housewares that my Father had given us that they started breaking. Anything valuable they could find or pull out of drawers they were breaking. I followed them and was able to snatch a few things from them to keep from getting broken. My Father was in another room working, from the dining room I could see him in his office which was on the same floor off of the dining room. I tried to get His attention so He could help us.*

## Real Life

I had been doing this business and ministry for 8 years, with minimal problems. Just a few easily solved disputes every couple of years. I just took it to church elders, and usually it worked out. Or I just took a loss. I've been defrauded a few times, no big deal (1 Corinthians 7).

All of the sudden it seemed like the game switched on me.

Part of it came from confusion. Babylon means "confusion." Ever since my supporters left to start a new brand, things got confusing. I would try and work with people I had worked with for years, and they would ask me if I was working with my former supporters. People whom I had worked with before began ignoring me.

A couple months later I got another supporter and ended up planning another major concert. I was excited about it. My wife was pregnant with our first child. My two-year contract at the school I was working at was coming to an end. I was looking forward to hitting the streets that summer and really making progress toward full time ministry.

I had a signed a contract to book a concert with a particular artist, paid the deposit, only to find out that they had given the event to my former supporters, because they thought they were working with me.

We ended up getting a makeup concert for the mixup, and promoted one of our most successful shows ever. Even in the street promotion souls were saved and impacted.

We also started a new Christian club series for fellowship and restarted the prayer parties, in order to prepare for the house of prayer... At this point I think I made it through a really tough test. I'm thinking that finally things will come together. We have some flyers designed that are more like gospel tracts for a major concert promotion. These tracts expose the enemy's lies in hip hop music, as well as invite people to our next major show.

Immediately we get squeezed to the point of death financially. That sounds dramatic but that's what it felt like. Things start breaking down, and nothing is working out. Not promotion, not a job, not business, nothing.

Then later on in that season, things got even worse. A greater percentage of my business relationships went bad. I started noticing patterns, the same things happening over and over again, with people that did not even know each other. When I started noticing the patterns is when I knew that I was experiencing was a spiritual attack.

All of the sudden there was hypocrisy, usury, baits & switches, good cop/bad cop games, and manipulative psychological techniques instead of the simple, straightforward kingdom business I had been used to doing for the past eight years. I don't know why it all changed. It just did.

Throughout all this, I'm still doing the work and glorifying God. We are still seeking to promote through different events and outreaches.

I was promised a particular concert at one price. They put an interest percentage into the contract without telling me. I missed it for a couple of reasons. One, I rushed in signing the contract because I didn't want to lose it like I lost the last one. Two, interest was never in anything else I had ever done with them. I had read and took detailed notes on all their contracts before, their business practices were usually very simple and straightforward. A month later when I caught it they said they would change it back to what they quoted me. Another month later they said they would change it back again. A couple weeks later they said the usury would stay in the contract, and if I didn't want to do it, my competitor was going to do it, so make a decision in two days.

I had already promised my new investor a certain level return based on the original price they quoted me. This price change squeezed everything, and would almost make me work just for the gas money I would use promoting the concert, as well as limit my flexibility to spend money on the outreaches and evangelism-based advertising leading up to the concert.

I got into promoting the kingdom of God to help preach a revival starting message, preach the gospel, and to eventually be able to raise money for a Christian fellowship facility and house of prayer, not to pay interest to a record label. I had been faithful in sowing to many different artists and ministries, paying in full, and taking losses in full for 8 years – and then all of the sudden I have to pay large interest on a profit? This was not right at all.

Imagine you went to a restaurant, and paid for your family to eat... The meal costs $39.50, according to the menu. After you finish, the waitress came back and gave you the bill, and it said it was 89.50. She says "Oops, thats a typo, I'll change that for you." You gave her your debit card, but when she came back the receipt says you were charged 89.50 anyway. Then she gets her manager and he says "Too bad, it was 89.50, stop wasting my time." Would you enjoy eating at that restaurant?

Imagine you buy a car from the same dealership every 5 years... And you always pay cash. After buying 3 previous cars from them, you think you are very familiar with the dealership. One year you come with $8000 to buy the car of your choice. You see it, and go to sign the familiar paperwork. Then you hand them 8000 cash, which they say is the price of the car. Then 3 months later you get a bill in the mail for an additional 2000. "We no longer accept just cash only, you have to pay a 25% interest rate even if you pay cash for your car. We didn't tell you because we knew you weren't used to paying that. So we told you the car was $8000, but really it's $8000 +25% if it lasts longer than 3 months." That's not just simply a higher price, that's a whole different class of transaction! Would you enjoy buying a car from a dealership that you couldn't trust?

That's kind of like the situation I was in. By this time I was so disgusted with the confusion and competition I had been dealing with for the past year, and the ways of Babylon among the body of Christ. I was very disappointed in the character of some of the believers I had worked with and I was disappointed in the acceptance of worldly business ethics and practices in ministry. I really just wanted to disconnect from the situation and try again later for a different event. So I cancelled my promotion of the concert and gave my investor his money back.

In the tough times for my family that followed... Sometimes I did wish that I had just "took the money and run." But in hindsight, I'm glad that I was guided by my integrity. The integrity of the upright shall guide them (Proverbs 11:3).

I not only kept myself from violating scriptures on business that would have corrupted my ministry, but I also disconnected myself from ministries that were on a downward spiral spiritually... And that went on to become more and more corrupted as time went on. Pretty soon the same artists that used to stand for holiness were off into the deep end and started doing obviously corrupt music and corrupt business, partnering with the world system to lead God's people astray. They were signing to ungodly labels, doing albums and songs with ungodly artists, and spreading spiritual corruption into a generation that was headed towards holiness.

So with spiritual insight, I'm glad I wasn't the one that changed. I stayed preaching the same message and standing for the same standard in ministry and in business. I wasn't the one that changed my goals. I wasn't the one that changed from a scriptural standard in business. I didn't change my strategy and make the glory of God's Word less important than profits. I didn't sacrifice truth for branding and popularity, I sacrificed branding and popularity for truth. My ministry goals stayed exactly the same since 2001 - promotion of the Word of God with words and music, and building a house of prayer. I just had to fine tune my strategy.

I knew that God was just using these challenges to strengthen me and show me how corrupt the world really is, and how easy it is for the world to corrupt the Church if we're not careful.

But on the natural side, things were very hard. I'm applying for jobs daily, can't find anything. No consistent income, even my dj gigs are a struggle, several people decide not to pay for work already done, contracts switched on us, gigs cancelled... all while my wife is pregnant with our first child. I have NEVER experienced anything like this all at once. We are dealing with multiple broken contracts, baits & switches; and several people have flipped the script on us.

Ever since I was laid off, I had been focused on developing the ministry God gave me. I hadn't used my degree in 5 years, so no corporate jobs are responding to my applications. I applied for all types of jobs, and the minimum wage jobs are ignoring me probably because I'm overqualified. I am thankful that God always supplied our needs through it all... But it was not fun at all, living life on the brink for some time.

This was a horrible season. I won't even lie, I was depressed. Things were totally weird. I felt beat up spiritually, and emotionally, and it affected my family and finances in a horrible way. It was a perfect storm, and a tremendous squeeze. Little income, baby on the way, and all these demons trying to manipulate and steal and destroy everything I have. I didn't know how to deal with this, because people had never really acted like this on this level before. Several people that I had no problems with in the past just flipped the script.

By the end of this I've learned by experience that we wrestle not against people, but against principalities and powers. So instead of arguing with people or fighting, I just try to seek God, move on, and figure out what to do the best I can.

On the positive side, this was a good time of pattern recognition. I began to recognize patterns in snake business tactics. I also began to recognize the patterns of attacks from the enemy that only came when I made progress towards **greater preaching** and **greater prayer**. I'm growing in wisdom and God begins to download the blueprints and plans for **greater victory**.

But it's still looking grim in the natural. I'm continually fighting thoughts of despair with the Word of God. Satan is pulling out everything on us and it's literally overwhelming. Though I fight depression constantly, I still hold out my faith that God must be about to do something HUGE that terrifies the enemy.

## Scripture

> *James 3: 16 For where envying and strife is, there is* <u>*confusion*</u> *and* <u>*every evil work.*</u>

**Babel or Babylon:** confusion (by mixing).

> *Revelations 17:1 Come hither ; I will shew unto thee the judgment of the great whore that sitteth upon many waters: 2* **With whom the** <u>**kings of the earth have committed fornication**</u> **,** *and the* <u>*inhabitants of the earth have been made drunk with the wine of her fornication*</u>*. 3 So he carried me away in the spirit into the wilderness: and I saw a woman sit upon a scarlet coloured beast, full of names of blasphemy, having seven heads and ten horns. 4 And the woman was arrayed in purple and scarlet colour, and decked with gold and precious stones and pearls, having a golden cup in her hand full of abominations and filthiness of her* <u>*fornication*</u>*: 5 And upon her forehead was a name written , MYSTERY, BABYLON THE GREAT, THE MOTHER OF HARLOTS AND ABOMINATIONS OF THE EARTH.*

Part of what the "Babylon Mother of Harlots" represents is a system of sinful business practices that political leaders and wealthy rulers get involved with. It's related to politics and religion, and from looking at Revelations 17 and 18 you can see that the system is primarily financial. This system affects the inhabitants of the earth as well. The system of Babylon is also responsible for the death of all God's saints, martyrs, apostles, prophets (Revelations 17:6, Revelations 18:20, 24).

In the Old and New Testament, God refers to this spiritually as fornication. Do the research in the Old Testament prophetic books. When God talks about kings and their wicked political and business practices, he calls it fornication - and it wasn't just physical.

> *Revelations 18:3 For all nations have drunk of the wine of the wrath of her fornication, and <u>the kings of the earth have committed fornication with her, and the merchants of the earth are waxed rich through the abundance of her delicacies</u>. 4 And I heard another voice from heaven, saying, Come out of her, my people, that ye be not partakers of her sins, and that ye receive not of her plagues.*

Yes, it's true that children of the world are wiser in some of their ways than the children of light (Luke 16). But all true business wisdom comes from God. God is the source of even the wisdom that the world uses.

The question becomes: which business principles that the world uses are biblical wisdom? Which practices are based in the lies of satan?

## God's Business is Simple

Business is basically an organized form of working, giving, and property management. God has instructions for business people.

> *Romans 12:8 ...He that giveth, let him <u>do it with simplicity</u>; he that ruleth, with diligence.*

Work, Get Paid.

> *Proverbs 14:23 In <u>all labour there is profit</u>: but the talk of the lips tendeth only to penury.*

Invest, Get return.

> *Galatians 6:7 Be not deceived; God is not mocked: for whatsoever a man soweth, that shall he also reap.*

Make Covenant, Keep Covenant, even if it hurts.

> *Psalms 15:4 He that sweareth to his own hurt , and changeth not.*

Creating business plans that are simple and generous will cause you to be stable.

> *Isaiah 32:7 The instruments also of the churl [rude miserly person] are evil: <u>he deviseth wicked devices to destroy the poor with lying words</u>, even when the needy speaketh right. 8 But <u>the liberal deviseth liberal[generous] things; and by liberal things shall he stand.</u>*

Allow others to make money on your business, even the poor.

> *Leviticus 19:9 And when ye reap the harvest of your land, <u>thou shalt not wholly reap the corners of thy field,</u> neither shalt thou gather the gleanings of thy harvest. 10 And <u>thou shalt not glean thy vineyard, neither shalt thou gather every grape</u> of thy vineyard; <u>thou shalt leave them for the poor and stranger</u>: I am the LORD your God.*

### Snake Business Tactics – Small Snakes and Big Snakes

Everybody makes mistakes. Not everybody that makes a mistake is a snake. The snake manifests when they refuse to make it right or take a loss for their mistake.

### SMALL SNAKES Bite & Poison:

## Lies/Unfaithfulness/Broken Agreements

God said that lies and broken covenants will increase in the last days.

> *2 Timothy 3:3 Without natural affection, <u>trucebreakers</u>, false accusers, incontinent, fierce, despisers of those that are good.*

## Double Tongue

When someone says two contradictory things out of one mouth, in order to gain advantage.

"I'm not going to smack you in the face (while smacking you in the face)."

"We don't want to stop you from making money" "But you can't make this... can't make that... can't do that."

## Disrespectful Communication

Accusing you of wrongdoing or wrong motives to put you on the defensive, gain an advantage, or cover up their mistake.

## Psychological Manipulation

Psychological manipulation is when someone uses scorn, despising, reproach, sarcasm, false accusations, discrediting, name-calling, threats, or dishonest communication to gain an advantage and control over someone else.

"You just don't know what you're doing."

"You're just trying to make a name for yourself."

"I'm disappointed in you because of (false accusation)."

Read the techniques of Sanballat and Tobiah in Nehemiah 2, 4, 6, and 13.

> *Nehemiah 2:19 But when Sanballat the Horonite, and Tobiah the servant, the Ammonite, and Geshem the Arabian, heard it, they laughed us to scorn , and despised us, and said , What is this thing that ye do ? will ye rebel against the king?*

> *Nehemiah 4:2 And he spake before his brethren and the army of Samaria, and said , What do these feeble Jews? will they fortify themselves? will they sacrifice? will they make an end in a day? will they revive the stones out of the heaps of the rubbish which are burned?*

> *Nehemiah 4:11 And our adversaries said, they shall not know, neither see, till we come in the midst among them, and slay them, and cause the work to cease.*

## Logical Fallacies

Logical fallacy is when people justify their false actions with nonsensical logic.

"This is just standard." (But the standard is wrong).

"It's always done like this." (And it's not right).

## Brand Warfare

Seeking ways to drag down someone else's name to gain advantage for yourself.

> *Psalms 15:3 He that <u>backbiteth not with his tongue,</u> nor doeth evil to his neighbour, nor taketh up a reproach against his neighbour.*

Take up a reproach = carry a scornful or negative campaign.

## Externalized Losses

If you make a mistake, you lose. If I make a mistake, you lose again!

I won't clean up after myself. Everybody else pays for my error. A corporate example of this would be a business that pollutes the community, causes diseases among the people, and then does nothing within their own company to fix it or make it right.

## BIG SNAKES Wrap & Squeeze:

## False Balance

Charging one person one thing and another person another, for the same product, because you think the other person has more money.

Changing your measuring balance to shift the weight of the transaction in your favor.

> *Proverbs 20:23* <u>*Divers weights are an* **abomination** *unto the LORD*</u>*; and a false balance is not good.*

## Bait & Switch

This is when someone promises one thing to get an agreement, then change what they promised.

No other story in the bible illustrates this as much as the story in Genesis of Jacob who labored seven years to marry Laban's daughter Rachel. After the seven years Laban tricked Jacob and gave him his daughter Leah to wife instead.

> *Genesis 27:25 So it came to pass in the morning, that behold, it was Leah. And he said to Laban, "What is this you have done to me? Was it not for Rachel that I served you? Why then have you deceived me?"*

## Good Cop/Bad Cop

This is when negotiators work in multiples, and you have to work with and talk to more than one person to get any decisions made. They play mistakes off of each other and switch roles with each other. This causes confusion and miscommunication in decision making.

## Usury

> *Proverbs 28:8 He that by* <u>*usury*</u> *and unjust gain increaseth his substance, he shall gather it for him that will pity the poor.*

### Usury:
1. (Qal) to bite
2. (Piel) to bite, to pay, give interest, lend for interest or usury
3. (Hiphil) to make to give interest

Interest is a financial share of a business or financial transaction. Usually you lay claim to that financial share by placing an investment in the transaction. When you demand to receive a percentage of profit above the level of your investment, it's called charging interest.

### INTEREST:
1 *a (1)* : right, title, or legal share in something *(2)* : participation in advantage and responsibility *b* : BUSINESS, COMPANY
2 *a* : **a charge** for borrowed money generally a percentage of the amount borrowed *b* : the **profit in goods or money that is made on invested** capital *c* : **an excess above what is due** or expected <returned the insults with *interest*>

## Slavery and Defrauding

Creating systems where you make money unjustly off of other people's work, and don't pay them justly. Rich men that create and profit off of these systems will end up with the most misery in the afterlife. Literally every dollar that they make unjustly will be a witness against them in judgment. That's a place you absolutely do not want to be – standing before God with every unjust dollar that you earned actually screaming "This Man is Wicked!!!"

> *James 5:1 Go to now, <u>ye rich men, weep and howl for your miseries that shall come upon you</u>. 2 Your riches are corrupted , and your garments are motheaten. 3 Your gold and silver is cankered ; and <u>the rust of them shall be a witness against you, and shall eat your flesh as it were fire.</u> Ye have heaped treasure together for the last days. 4 Behold , the <u>hire of the labourers who have reaped down your fields, which is of you kept back by fraud , crieth</u> : and the cries of them which have reaped are entered into the ears of the Lord of sabaoth.*

There are many systems of unjust slavery that men operate, and they have grown more and more sophisticated as time progresses. **Chattel slavery** (as opposed to indentured servanthood or employment which is biblical) relegates men below the image of God. It is an affront to God. **Sociological and Political slavery** is similar; it uses unjust laws to make one people group financially subservient to another by trapping them in geological or financial boundaries based on their race or class. **Financial slavery**, which includes promoting debt, as well as the debasement and control of currency to keep people in perpetual debt, can be the most insidious of them all.

## Business Laws and Standards based on Lies

When we replace God's rules and standards with the ever-changing precepts of men, we defile the earth. Our business schools and law schools and universities used to be founded upon the Bible, literally. In the 1860s after Darwin introduced his lies to the culture, men began to change the rules of science, law, and business.

> *Isaiah 24:5 The <u>earth also is defiled</u> under the inhabitants thereof; because they have <u>transgressed the laws, changed the ordinance, broken the everlasting covenant</u>.*

Now, instead of starting from the foundation of an unchanging standard, many laws are subject to special interpretation and changed from a case-to-case basis. Political and Business leaders learn by case studies more than they learn principles.

## SOLUTIONS TO SNAKE BUSINESS

### Simplicity in Communication

> *Matthew 5:37 But let your communication be, Yea, yea; Nay, nay: for <u>whatsoever is more than these cometh of evil.</u>*

Jesus said "Let your yes be yes, and let your no be no.... ANYTHING MORE THAN THAT COMES FROM THE EVIL ONE"

All of the psychological manipulation and manipulative negotiation tactics in the world of Babylon business come from the evil one. Communication that is not straightforward, honest, loving, and truthful comes from evil.

In the multitude of words, there is no lack of sin (Proverbs 10:19). When words are multiplied and things are made more complicated than they should be, it's because there is sin and evil inside of the communication.

## Straightforward Talk

What do you do when you need to communicate more than yes/no? Ask questions. Give straightforward answers.

> *Proverbs 25:8 Go not forth hastily to strive, lest thou know not what to do in the end thereof, when thy neighbour hath put thee to shame. 9 Debate thy cause with thy neighbour himself; and discover not a secret to another: 10 Lest he that heareth it put thee to shame , and thine infamy turn not away.*

Avoid disrespectful talk. The root word of "sarcasm" is 'caustic', which means bitter.

> *Proverbs 22:10 Cast out the scorner, and contention shall go out ; yea, strife and reproach shall cease. 11 He that loveth pureness of heart, for the grace of his lips the king shall be his friend.*

Communicate completely, and communicate visually.

## Simplicity in Transactions

> *Romans 12:8 ...He that giveth, let him do it with simplicity; he that ruleth, with diligence.*

God said to give with simplicity. Business transactions should be simple, not complicated.

> *Psalms 15:5 He that putteth not out his money to usury, nor taketh reward against the innocent. He that doeth these things shall never be moved.*

## Faithful Actions

Be faithful, stick to your commitment. Even if keeping your word harms your cause, do everything you can to fulfill your agreements.

> *Psalms 15:4 In whose eyes a vile person is contemned; but he honoureth them that fear the LORD. He that sweareth to his own hurt , and changeth not.*

## Look for Character and Simplicity

Just "getting it on paper" is not enough when people break contracts and agreements all the time. Look for people whose only boast is in the Scriptures, humility, and God's wisdom, not in their worldly experience or success. This has more to do with **character** and **simplicity** (Romans 12:8) than it does with having to hire a lawyer for every transaction. I have learned that the one who is trying to overcomplicate a simple transaction is the one who is trying to take advantage.

## The Key to Business and Economic Development

> *Proverbs 9:10 The fear of the LORD is the beginning of wisdom: and the knowledge of the holy is understanding.*

**wisdom: chokmah**
1. wisdom
2. skill (in war)
3. wisdom (in administration)
4. shrewdness, wisdom
5. wisdom, prudence (in religious affairs)
6. wisdom (ethical and religious)

> *Proverbs 8:12 I wisdom dwell with prudence, and find out knowledge of witty inventions. 13 The fear of the*

> LORD is to <u>hate evil:</u> pride, and arrogancy, and the
> evil way, and the froward mouth, do I hate.

The fear of the Lord is to hate evil. Hating evil gives you wisdom. Wisdom is skill and creativity in problem solving. When you have wisdom and you mix it with diligence in your natural talents and interests, you will make creative progress. Wisdom dwelling with prudence finds out knowledge of witty inventions, and new creativity.

The key to economic and business development is the fear of the Lord, which is the beginning of wisdom. We need people who are afraid of God's judgments so that they will do what's right instead of doing what's wrong. We need people who don't want to hurt people or harm God's earth, because those people will get wisdom to create new products and services that will benefit the community, not harm it.

Anything less is just a scam.

### Interpretation

The dreams represented me playing a game (business) with those whom I thought had integrity... but really their ideas of business came from the world, not from scripture.

The principalities or demons (not the people involved) sought to destroy precious things in our household. But God was downstairs working on our biggest blessing anyway, our son!

Previously, I had experienced being defrauded in business maybe once every couple years. In this season, it was a lot more often. One day after this time I literally had an epiphany! When I looked back, it was always the people who had pride in their worldly experience that ended up defrauding me. People who did business the kingdom way did not boast in their worldly experiences.

In my 10 years of ministry, I found out that whenever I dealt with someone who had pride in their worldly accomplishments, they were the ones that did wrong. I was embarrassed that it took me 9 years to recognize the pattern. *"I did this secular before I got saved." "I did this for big labels before I got saved." "I do this for big corporations." "I've got this or that business degree."*

I'm not saying it's wrong to get a business degree or have secular business experience. I'm saying it's wrong to take pride in those things and lean on worldly wisdom instead of scriptural wisdom. I've worked with many people who had great success in the world but were humble instead of arrogant. The difference is night & day!

There's a false separation between business and ministry. Business, or property management, labor, and exchange, is actually scriptural. Ministers work with so-called business-minded people to handle the business "side." That's fine if the business minded person gets their business wisdom from scripture. But when they work with a business minded person who is prideful because of their worldly experiences, then most likely some of their ways and techniques will end up becoming corrupted and sinful, and they won't even know it.

In the Old and New Testament, God refers to worldly and sinful business alliances and techniques as spiritual fornication and spiritual harlotry; this is what the prostitutes represented in the dream.

We have to understand what the Bible speaks about those who have **"a heart exercised in covetous practices (2 Peter 2:14)"** In the world system, some schools, businesses, and even sports leagues actually **train** you on how to use snake business techniques and psychological warfare tactics that were discussed in this chapter. In the Body of Christ we must purge ourselves of the ungodly strategies we used to **get more and more and gain advantage over others** (Jude 1:16) when we were in the world system.

Jesus said that we should be as wise as a **serpent** (knowing how snakes operate), and as harmless as a **dove,** because *He sends us into the world system as sheep among wolves* (Matthew 10:16). Unfortunately, I was not as wise as the serpents at that time. But by the grace of God I know I'm a **sheep**, not a **wolf**.

I count it as an honor that once things went corrupt, I was separated. For me it was never about just the music, and I was never a star-stuck fan. So while it was hard to see things go south spiritually, it was easy to disconnect with corruption, because spiritual corruption could never bring revival, and that's what my heart was really after.

## Application

**The spirit of Babylon, inspired by demons, comes with worldly business practices over scripture.**

Keep communication simple.

Keep transactions simple.

Study business according to the Word of God, and interpret everything through the lense of the business scriptures of the bible. Don't assume that because something is "normal," that it is Godly.

Anyone that is a braggadocio about what they did in the world or for secular or major businesses or labels - (even in Christian Music) watch out. **Pride is an indicator**. Some of their ways may be evil.

**Use Your Gift of Discerning of Spirits** (1 Corinthians 12) - It's a gift from the Holy Ghost. You know it. There were times when I knew someone was shady but my rational mind said "They are a Christian; they won't do anything wrong, it will all work out"

What to do when snakebitten: shake it off and move on like Apostle Paul (Acts 28:5).

Confess that the snakebite won't affect you, it will only make you stronger. Any deadly poison will not harm you (James 3:8, Mark 16:18).

Love your enemies. Bless them that curse you. **Lend, hoping for nothing in return. (Luke 6:35)**

**How to forgive: Forgiving debts means that someone who owed you something now owes you nothing**. In order to forgive, you have to continually say that the person who owed you love, money, or a promise, "no longer owes me anything."

If you don't replace your desire "for giving" then you can never "forgive." Instead, you have to get what you are owed directly from God. Look to God to supply what you lost!

**Pull on God to give you what you need,** instead of on the person who didn't keep their promise, or who stole from you. God will end up giving you seven times what they took (Proverbs 7).

**Purify Your Ministry from all secular influences that cannot be sourced from scripture.**

**When the Body of Christ rises above the ways of Babylon's confusion - by executing simple, faithful, and generous business - God will bless us greatly, and we will see a great financial windfall come through us for God's purposes. Purity will bring increase!**

# 6

## CRIMINALS IN THE HOUSE OF PRAYER

**Enemy Profile:** Criminals and thieves in the Church steal God's worship and prayer, turning the House of God into a place of buying and selling, where they can hide.

**Shereena's Dream**

*Hit in the Mouth: May 2011*

*Esosa was standing in the lobby of a large church near the church bookstore. He was standing next to a muscular, African American man, the man was very angry. The man had muscles all over his body, his body almost looked deformed because he had muscles bulging all over his neck, chest, arms hands, and legs. He face was disfigured with anger, he looked like a monster. Two older African American men and a woman, who represented church authorities, had the man in handcuffs with his arms behind his back because he was a criminal. The strong angry man forcefully broke free of the hand cuffs and quickly punched Esosa in the mouth. Esosa stood there with his mouth bleeding, with broken teeth. The blow to his mouth was so strong, his mouth was now deformed. Esosa just stood there, with his head bobbing around. The church authorities did not do anything to reprimand the criminal. They held the criminal's arms loosely behind his back, and followed him as he led them around the church doing whatever he pleased. The criminal had the freedom to do whatever he pleased in the church. The church authorities pretended to have the criminal under control, and they could have subdued him even though he was strong. But they did not want to. They pretended to restrain him, but they actually enjoyed the criminal's company and were on his side. He was almost like their pet. But they had to make it seem as if they were restraining him. In the dream the criminal led the church authorities to the church music studio, the criminal was working on music in the church. In the last scene of the dream I was sitting down on the border of a cement pond. Esosa came to me. I remember feeling so bad for him when I saw his face, his mouth was severely disfigured and crooked. His speech was slurred from the impact of the blow from the criminal. Esosa laid his head on my chest, and said "I just want to talk to you about the Martin Luther King mission that I have". He wanted me to talk about his mission with him. He was so discouraged, and the weight of the mission was heavily on his heart and mind, so much so that he could barely hold his physical body upright. He also wanted to talk to me about the house of prayer. We sat together and I held him, and tried to give him comfort and rest.*

## Real Life

After all the drama happened with the promotions, we still worked on our smaller events and prayer events. Life is still a struggle, but our new son is coming any day, so that gives us hope. We believe that God is going to turn things around.

Soon after that my former youth pastor invited me to a meeting where a large group of churches were planning to work together to evangelize the whole Metro Detroit Area over a 40-day period. It was about Unity and Citywide Evangelism, so of course I loved it immediately, and committed to helping and promoting the effort in any way possible. It reminded me of what I had been a part of at MSU. Unity and Citywide Evangelism is part of the spiritual DNA of our ministry... so we were excited to be a part.

One of the ways we assisted the work was by facilitating 80 days of night and day prayer for the effort. We already had the prayer events going, and we already planned on building a house of prayer in the city, so it was a perfect fit. We wanted to build a wall of unified, citywide prayer in Detroit that would be 24-7.

Many people supported and helped out. We focused completely on building the house of prayer for a while, and God did some amazing things. Though we have not yet made it to 24-7, we still were able to fulfill our part faithfully. The work still continues!

## Scripture

Jesus's most violent acts were against people that turned His Father's House of prayer into a den of thieves.

> *Matthew 21:12 And Jesus went into the temple of God, and cast out all them that sold and bought in the temple, and overthrew the tables of the moneychangers, and the seats of them that sold doves. 13 And said unto them, "It is written, My House shall be called the House of Prayer, but you have made it a den of thieves." 14 And the blind and the lame came to him the temple, and He healed them.*

We pray that Jesus Christ would march into His Church again and make it into a House of Prayer for every nation, every ethnic group. We pray that He would cast out moneychangers and turn over tables. We also pray that the blind and the lame would come and be healed.

After we repent, the Church will not be the best example of racial division every Sunday. But to do that, we need to become a House of Prayer for every ethnic group. Racial division is a huge stronghold in the world. It should not be so in Jesus Christ. Soon we will be the world's best example of unity!

When we cleanse the temple, get the thieves out, and rebuild the tabernacle of David, this will happen. Not only will the world see Unity, but the healing power of God will rise up again. When we become a House of Prayer, Jesus will come and miraculous healing will take place. The blind will see, and the lame will walk.

The House of Prayer was a reference to the Tabernacle that David built for God in the Old Testament. It was a place where prayer, praise and worship went up before God day & night. Musicians, Singers, Porters, and others were employed to worship God and facilitate prayer.

> *1 Chronicles 9:33 And these are the singers, chief of the fathers of the Levites, who remaining in the chambers were free: <u>for they were employed in that work day and night</u>.*

> **1 Chronicles 15:16 And David spake to the chief of the Levites to appoint their brethren to be the singers with instruments of musick, psalteries and harps and cymbals, sounding, by lifting up the voice with joy.**

## God Requires PRAYER + UNITY for His WORD to Have Maximum Effect on the World

> *2 Chronicles 7:14 If My People, who are called by My name, will **humble themselves, and pray**, and seek my face, and turn from their wicked ways... Then I will hear from heaven, forgive their sin, and I will <u>heal their land</u>.*

> *John 17:20-21 Neither pray I for these alone, but for them also which shall believe on me through their word; **That they all may be one**; as thou, Father, art in me, and I in thee, that they also may be one in us: **that the world may believe** <u>that thou hast sent me</u>.*

## Night & Day Prayer Yields Results

## All of the major prophetic promises of God are linked to Night & Day Prayer:

1.  Harvest of the Gentiles is connected to the Tabernacle of David (Night & Day prayer & worship, also see Psalms 132-134,):

> *Acts 15:16 After this I will return , and will build again the <u>tabernacle of David,</u> which is fallen down; and I will build again the ruins thereof, and I will set it up: 17 <u>That the residue of men might seek after the Lord, and all the Gentiles,</u> upon whom my name is called, saith the Lord, who doeth all these things.*

2.  City Transformation is Given in Context of Night & Day Prayer:

> *Isaiah 62:6 I have set <u>watchmen upon thy walls,</u> O Jerusalem, which shall <u>never hold their peace day nor night:</u> ye that make mention of the LORD, <u>keep not silence, watchmen</u> 7 And give him no rest, till he establish, and till he make Jerusalem a praise in the earth.*

3.  Speedy Justice from God is connected to night & day prayer:

> *Luke 18:7 And shall not God avenge his own elect, which **cry day and night** <u>unto him,</u> though he bear long with them? 8 I tell you that he will avenge them speedily. Nevertheless when the Son of man cometh, <u>**shall he find faith on the earth**</u>?*

4.  Even the first arrival of Jesus the Messiah was connected to the Night & Day prayers of Anna the Prophetess, and Simeon the Priest:

> *Luke 2:36 And there was one Anna, a prophetess, the daughter of Phanuel, of the tribe of Aser: she was of a great age , and had lived with an husband seven years from her virginity; 37 And she was a widow of about fourscore and four years, which <u>departed not</u>*

*from the temple, but **served God with fastings and prayers night and day.***

## Real Unity – One Mind on Jesus, One Mouth on Christ

One thing we need to pray about is Unity in the Church. Unity is actually Jesus the King's #1 evangelism strategy. He prayed that we would be one, so that the world could believe in Him.

But what is real unity? Real Biblical Unity is not ecumenicalism, it's not putting aside our beliefs. It's not necessarily everybody joining the same organization, or sitting in the same building at one time. True Unity is conforming our beliefs to the image of Christ and the Word of God. Real unity is found in Romans 15.

> *Romans 15:6 That ye may with <u>one mind and one mouth</u> glorify God, even the Father of our Lord Jesus Christ.*

**One Mind** – Thinking the same things about Jesus Christ.

**One Mouth** – Saying the same things about Jesus Christ.

When we look at Jesus Christ long and hard enough in His Word and by His Spirit, we will all start seeing the same glorious and beautiful things about Him. Then we will be changed into His image. We will stop fighting about our different roles, and see each other connected to Christ. We will chop off every false head, principality, stronghold or idol that leads us away from Him. We won't be in disagreement about Jesus - we will be in agreement with Jesus and about Jesus.

Every ministry will think the same things about Jesus. Every ministry will say the same things about Jesus Christ. That's true Unity.

## Bringing Down Dividing Walls of Hostility

Jesus Christ is bringing down the dividing walls of hostility between Jew and Gentile, black and white, baptist and pentecostal, calvinist and charismatic, and every other unnecessary division in His Body. We are praying that God would continue to **desegregate His Church** so that we can show the world that He sent Jesus (John 17).

> *Ephesians 2:13 But now in Christ Jesus ye who sometimes were far off are made nigh by the blood of Christ. 14 For he is our peace, who hath made both one, and hath **broken** down **the middle** wall **of** partition **between us**; 15 Having abolished in his flesh the **enmity**, even the law of commandments contained in ordinances; for to make in himself of twain one \*new man, so making peace; 16 And that he might reconcile both unto God in one body by the cross, having slain the **enmity** thereby\*: 17 And came and preached peace to you which were afar off, and to them that were nigh. 18 For through him we both have access by one Spirit unto the Father.*

**Jesus Christ is slaying the enmity** and breaking down the middle walls of partition in His Church. He is making His body one. His Body will no longer be dismembered, but re-membered. We will remember and rightly discern the Lord's Body. God also wants to desegregate denominations, organizations, and movements.

There is coming a time when we will understand our different callings, and honor our different callings. There is coming a time very soon when we will play our different roles as ONE team, not team versus team. When Jesus is lifted high, and everyone's eye is on Him, this will happen.

**God also is uniting Jew and Gentile.** God is raising up African, European, Asian, Native American, and Middle Eastern believers who will see Jews as potential family members, while the world is persecuting them. Jews will join Gentiles as one new man in Christ, when the Church begins to take up the same burden and passion that Paul had in Romans 11 – to see the Jews saved. They will pray for them, love them, and preach to them until the work is done. Then when the Jews are saved, Jesus the Messiah will come back to take over the earth, and we can get on with the universe! Let it be so now! Come quickly Lord Jesus, Amen.

### Building Up A Wall of Unified Prayer – Nehemiah

If you go back and look at the book of Nehemiah, you see that God used him to inspire each family in Jerusalem to rebuild their section of the wall of Jerusalem. This is similar to what God is doing now, in all the cities of the earth. God is inspiring churches, ministries, bands, singers, and intercessors, and preachers all over the earth to build night & day walls of prayer, worship, and intercession to God! Everyone takes a section, works together in Unity, and night & day prayer & worship goes up like incense before the throne of God.

What I want to point out is the covenant that they made with God after the wall was built. In Nehemiah chapter 10, they committed to:

1. Walk in God's Commandments (Nehemiah 10:29).
2. Avoid spiritual adultery and idolatry - by not marrying and mixing with foreign nations (Nehemiah 10:30).
3. To honor the Sabbath day and rest instead of exercise in commerce and trade (Nehemiah 10:31).
4. A financial commitment to give financially for the house of God, for the priest, the Levites, porters, and singers (Nehemiah 10:33-39).

After Nehemiah left and went back to the King of Babylon, the people of Jerusalem reverted back to their old ways. Let's look at the problems that showed up after a few years:

1. Tobiah (the main non-believing hater that persecuted Nehemiah while he was building the unified wall) had a room in the house of God. The provisions that were supposed to be given to the Levites, the singers, the porters, and the priests were given to Tobiah instead (Nehemiah 13:5).
2. The Levites had to go get regular jobs because their provision was not given to them (Nehemiah 13:10).
3. Jews were doing work on the Sabbath, and doing commerce with other nations on the Sabbath (Nehemiah 13:15, 16).
4. Jews had married foreign wives, and their children couldn't even speak the Jewish language (Nehemiah 13:23-24).

So when the cat was away, the mice started to play! Imagine if you had done all that work to restore God's city, and then as soon as you went away they undid every godly practice that God used you to establish. If you read the rest of Nehemiah 13, you will see that he got pretty violent and angry to restore what was lost.

Lord, raise up Nehemiah's in our day! Those who will build, and rebuild, and restore God's house with zeal.

## Interpretation

The things that Satan used to attack our ministry was to hinder the greater purpose of our ministry: Unity, Creative Evangelism, and Night & Day prayer. I noticed the pattern, that just as in 2006, the financial attacks were precursors to increased plans in prayer ministry and evangelism. All of my equipment was stolen when we first planned to introduce the prayer events and outreach projects. This season was no different. As we got closer to our plans for prayer and massive evangelism, our influence was attacked. The criminal hitting me in the mouth symbolized Satan attempting to steal and destroy my influence.

This is one reason I know that God was speaking through these dreams: I had never even talked to my wife about Martin Luther King. I don't even consider myself a fighter for civil rights. The desire for unity is my heart, mainly unity in the body of Christ, across denomination lines. However, if I seek unity in the body of Christ, I do also seek racial unity. For much of the division in the church is white church versus black church, and urban versus suburban. Many of our cities' roots of division have a lot to do with racism in the church. Selah...

It's also telling that in the dream the criminal worked in the area of music for the church. Much of the battle I was fighting was due to corruption in the Christian music industry, God's music being corrupted by worldly business practices. The House of Prayer that David built for God had much to do with musicians and singers worshipping God Day & Night. Jesus rebuked those in the temple of His day because they weren't a house of prayer, but a den of thieves. **Why**

**did Jesus contrast the House of Prayer with the Den of Thieves?** The thieves were in God's House to take the resources that were supposed to be dedicated to prayer.

## Application

**Pray aloud in the evening, morning, and noon** (Psalms 55). Become a House of Prayer in your own soul, because you are the Temple of God.

**Help build Unity in Truth and Night & Day Prayer** in your city and region.

**Realize that musical talents and gifts are purposed for worship, prayer, instruction, and testifying of the glory of God.**

Do whatever you can to turn God's house from a place where thieves can hide back into a house of prayer. Get the moneychangers out and the worshippers in.

**When it comes down to it; if we are not on the Wall of Unified and Citywide prayer, we can't expect much. But if we GET ON THE WALL... faith will rise! GOD will move with Power and Transformation.**

# 7

# GET YOUR DOGS OUT MY HOUSE!

**Enemy Profile:** Dogs use their tongues against others. Wolf-packs are ministry groups that use their tongues against others.

**Shereena's Dream**

*Dogs in Our House: July 2011*

*Esosa and I were walking through our condo looking it over. We had moved all of our belongings out and had just finished cleaning the condo. We had found a new place, so we were doing a final walk-through of the condo to be sure everything was clean before we left. We were walking into what used to be our bedroom when the front door burst open and two large, vicious Doberman Pinchers came into the condo barking ferociously, running through the apartment looking for us. The dogs were held on leashes by an invisible being. When we heard the dogs we ran through our room and out the window. When we got through the window we kept running because the dogs ran out the window after us. We got to the front of the condo buildings and ran into the street. The dogs kept trying to come after us, but when we got off of the condo property onto the street their leashes were suddenly yanked and they were attached to a garage that appeared, and the dogs could go no further. The dogs could not go off of the condo property. I had kept running and was halfway down the block when I stopped and realized the dogs were not chasing us anymore. I turned around and even though the dogs could not chase us anymore, they were still barking and jumping around trying to intimidate us. Esosa had stopped running and was finding sticks to hit the dogs with. He was trying to fight them even though they were restrained and could not come after him anymore. He was standing in front of them trying to fight them with sticks and anything he could find. I was standing half a block away watching him, wondering why he wouldn't just walk away, I did not know why he was still fighting the dogs since we did not need to go back to that condo, since we were already moving to a new place.*

### Real Life

We're still in a tough time period financially, and I'm starting to get some clues as to why.

Our last bit of consistent income is squeezed even tighter. At one of the schools that I substitute teach at, there are lies made up about me by kids I don't even know.

I also start to notice that people that used to work with me for concerts are ignoring me when I contact them. One actually told me they didn't want to work with me anymore. Then when I pressed and found out why, we cleared everything up easily. It was a misunderstanding based on a complaint that someone had.

I ask a buddy of mine to help me out with the house of prayer. A college friend of 12 years, he hesitated and initially didn't want to help me with the house of prayer because he heard a lie about me. "Word around the church is artists won't work with you anymore because you didn't pay someone." This was a lie.

This episode particularly perturbed me. Here I was, trying to forgive & forget, move on, and keep my mouth shut about the things that had been done to me. Satan doesn't care; he's still trying to stop me. I don't even know all what has been said about me, or who was saying it. I began to wonder just how much has been hindered with my ministry and family because of slander. Gossip (facts) and Slander (lies) are both sins, and they come from Satan.

I still hold on to my faith, and I know regardless that no weapon formed against me shall prosper, and every tongue that rises up against me I shall condemn. This is my heritage because I am a servant of God. I learned how Satan really works as an Accuser. Just like any bully or rapist, he won't stop as long as he can keep me quiet. I begin to realize that it's my responsibility to enforce my victory.

## Scripture

### Dogs

Which animal walks with their tongues out? Dogs. Their tongues walk around the earth (Psalms 73:9), they attack with their mouth (Psalms 140:3) and try to prevail with their tongue.

> *Psalms 12:3 The LORD shall cut off all flattering lips, and the tongue that speaketh proud things: 4 Who have said, <u>With our tongue will we prevail; our lips are our own: who is lord over us?</u>*

Paul had deceitful ministers that trailed his ministry to try to discredit him and steal his work. They would visit a church that Paul had established, and tell the people that Paul didn't really know what he was doing. Paul called these false apostles dogs.

> *Philippians 3:2 <u>Beware of dogs,</u> beware of evil workers, beware of the concision.*

David had dogs chasing him too, he wrote about them in the Psalms.

> *Psalms 59:1 Deliver me from mine enemies, O my God: defend me from them that rise up against me. 2 Deliver me from the workers of iniquity, and save me from bloody men. 3 For, lo, they lie in wait for my soul: the mighty are gathered against me; not for my transgression, nor for my sin, O LORD. 4 They run and prepare themselves without my fault: awake to help me, and behold. 5 Thou therefore, O LORD God of hosts, the God of Israel, awake to visit all the heathen: be not merciful to any wicked transgressors. Selah. 6 They return at evening: <u>they make a noise like a dog, and go round about the city.</u> 7 Behold, <u>they belch out with their mouth: swords are in their</u>*

> *lips: for who, say they, doth hear? 8 But thou, O LORD, shalt laugh at them; thou shalt have all the heathen in derision. 9 Because of his strength will I wait upon thee: for God is my defence. 10 The God of my mercy shall prevent me: God shall let me see my desire upon mine enemies. 11 Slay them not, lest my people forget: scatter them by thy power; and bring them down , O Lord our shield.*

At Jesus' crucifixion He was surrounded by dogs. They were dogs because they were not God's people, and they were dogs because of the way they were using their tongues.

> *Psalms 22:16 For dogs have compassed me: the assembly of the wicked have inclosed me: they pierced my hands and my feet. 20 Deliver my soul from the sword; my darling from the power of the dog.*

Symbolically, dogs are wicked and symbolize people that are not in God's Kingdom. We're not talking about "Fido," man's best friend here!

> *Revelations 22:15 For without are dogs, and sorcerers, and whoremongers, and murderers, and idolaters, and whosoever loveth and maketh a lie.*

David had dogs persecuting him. Paul had people following him around speaking negatively about his ministry. Jesus talked about dogs as well. These people who used their tongues and their mouths for evil were called dogs several times in scriptures. Don't be a dog! Use your tongue for blessing and not cursing.

## Wolves

Jesus sent us as sheep among wolves, so we have to be harmless, and gentle like doves. But we also have to be wise, careful and as calculating as serpents, but for the purpose of doing good, not evil.

> Matthew 10:16 Behold, I send you forth as sheep in the midst of wolves: be ye therefore wise as serpents, and harmless as doves.

A false prophet comes into the church looking like a sheep, but they don't speak for God, they only speak things that will help them make money, because they are ravening wolves, hungry to eat God's people.

> Matthew 7:15 Beware of false prophets, which come to you in sheep's clothing, but inwardly they are ravening wolves.

Paul knew that wolves would come to divide the church and make money by getting disciples for themselves with their own doctrines, and discrediting the biblical ministry of real apostles.

> Acts 20:29 For I know this, that after my departing shall grievous wolves enter in among you, not sparing the flock.

Wolf Packs - They like to clique up, they are carnal, they are marauders; they get together to devour others with their mouths.

Sometimes we think that God is like us, that our opinions are His. But His ways and thoughts are higher than ours.

> Psalms 50:19 Thou givest thy mouth to evil, and thy tongue frameth deceit. 20 Thou sittest and speakest against thy brother; thou slanderest thine own mother's son. 21 These things hast thou done , and I

> *kept silence; thou thoughtest that I was altogether such an one as thyself: but I will reprove thee, and set them in order before thine eyes.*

Wolves are similar to dogs... they followed Paul's team in packs. They took it as their responsibility to discredit and steal his ministry fruit.

We don't need any more wolf packs in the church – ministries whose specialty is tearing down and stealing from other ministries. This is part of division and denominational divides. How often have you heard preachers that always have to diss the "big church" or the "small church" or the "baptists" or the "charismatics" or "those calvinists" or "those noncalvinists." It's useless to tear down our brothers instead of building them up.

It's okay to reprove the works of darkness (Ephesians 5), but when we don't speak for God we turn into dogs and wolves. Speaking for God involves God's timing, God's place, God's responsibility, God's Scripture, and God's attitude. Publicly correcting false doctrine is not the same as dragging people's name down behind their back.

### How to Get the Dogs Out of Your House

Psalms 101 – Don't let them in your house in the first place. Cut off people who gossip. Don't tolerate them in your presence, because if you do, they will turn their tongues on you.

> *Psalms 101:1 I will sing of mercy and judgment: unto thee, O LORD, will I sing. 2 I will behave myself wisely in a perfect way. O when wilt thou come unto me? I will walk within <u>my house</u> with a perfect heart. 3 <u>I will set no wicked thing before mine eyes: I hate the work of them that turn aside; it shall not cleave to me</u>. 4 A froward heart shall depart from me: I will not know a wicked person. 5 <u>Whoso privily slandereth his neighbour, him will I cut off</u> : him that hath an high look and a proud heart will not I suffer. 6 Mine eyes shall be upon the faithful of the land, that they may*

> *dwell with me: he that walketh in a perfect way, he shall serve me. 7 He that worketh deceit shall not dwell within my house: <u>he that telleth lies shall not tarry in my sight.</u> 8 I will early destroy all the wicked of the land; that <u>I may cut off all wicked doers from the city of the LORD.</u>*

No weapon… formed against me… shall prosper… (Sing Fred!) But finish the rest, too.

> *Isaiah 54:17 No weapon that is formed against thee shall prosper; <u>and every tongue that shall rise against thee in judgment thou shalt condemn.</u> This is the heritage of the servants of the LORD, and their righteousness is of me, saith the LORD.*

Many people confess the first part of this scripture, but they ignore the second part. I realized that I would have to take part in my own victory when I figured out that the "b" section of this scripture required my action. I had to take authority and condemn the tongues which rose up in judgment against me. I was waiting for God to take action when I had the sword in my own hand.

Sometimes you will have to participate in your own deliverance from dogs by refusing to tolerate it and becoming angry about it.

> *Proverbs 25:23 The north wind driveth away rain: so doth an <u>angry countenance</u> backbiting tongue.*

## Interpretation

Dogs in our house symbolized the tongues of gossip and slander going out about the things that had happened to us. It was even trying to affect everything else we did as we tried to move on. I was fighting the dogs by myself, but soon after this dream occurred, and I explained it to her, my wife realized what was going on and we started to attack the problem together.

This revelation of dogs even gave more clarity on some dog dreams she had gotten when we first got married. We tightened up our own tongues, and raised our standard of the conversations we allowed in our presence. We realized that we would have to drive away the dogs ourselves by being on one accord and condemning the tongues that rose up against us.

## Application

**Getting the Dogs out of your house means fighting the tongues of wolves in sheep's clothing.**

Never allow your tongue to talk about others behind their back.

Always steer conversations away from dog-talk: "Let's not talk about him/her." "I don't want to talk about that."

Watch out for gossips and rebuke them quickly before they get too far into their talk.

Beware of people who always have something negative to say about others. Beware of dogs.

Avoid being with people that talk about the business of others.

Let's bind up the dogs and wolves within the Church, and loose a culture of:

**- Thanksgiving to others for what they have done**

**- Honoring others for who they are (not for who they aren't)**

**- Blessing others for the good qualities they have**

**- Praying for others**

**- Interceding for any of their deficiencies that we may notice**

When the Body of Christ stops pointing the finger and speaking vanity, and instead uses our tongues for edification in Love and declaring of Truth, we will rise in Authority and our Words will become more powerful.

# 8

# JEZEBEL 2.0 CHOPPING HER HEAD OFF

**Enemy Profile:** Jezebel 2.0 (New Covenant Jezebel) is much sneakier than Jezebel 1.0 (Jezebel before Christ Died & Rose). Instead of outright killing the prophets (upfront), she calls herself a prophetess, and then introduces spiritual fornication and idolatry into the Kingdom. This spirit seduces by looking successful and then teaches other ministers by example. Spiritual fornication and idolatry then leads to natural fornication, adultery, and divorce in the Church. Jezebel also produces spiritual miscarriages, children that are killed with death.

**Shereena's Dream**

*Woman Trying to Wound Me and Destroy Esosa – She Gets her Head Chopped Off : June 2011*

*I dreamed that Esosa and I were together in the same place but we were not next to each other. A spirit came, she looked like an ugly woman with an odd shape, she was very, VERY crazy and psychotic, she was also very dark. She came next to me, she had several little sharp tools she was trying to wound me with by poking me with them. The psychotic woman was laughing nervously as she did this. When she pulled out the tools and started poking me I immediately ran over to Esosa so he could protect me. I ran to him and told him what the woman was doing. The woman followed me. I grabbed Esosa's arm to try to hold on to him. He yanked his arm away, told me I was fine and walked away. He was busy doing other things. When he walked away the woman pulled out the tools again and for a second time started trying to wound me. Again I ran to Esosa and he walked away from me once more. When I was near*

*Esosa the woman would not stab me, but when Esosa walked away she would pull the tools out.*

*Then I saw the crazy woman in a garage that had big tools in it. She was trying to turn herself into a bomb to destroy Esosa. She was trying to wound me, but totally destroy Esosa. Esosa and I got together and realized what she was doing.*

*The woman was at a banquet for dignitaries, she was a guest at the banquet. She was dressed up, sitting at a table alone. Esosa and I saw her through the glass window in the door of the banquet room. We barged in with a very large sword and cut her head off in front of everyone.*

### Real Life

For a while we had been battling a spirit of depression. It would jump from me to my wife, back and forth. I would wake up a lot of mornings having to speak out against suicidal thoughts.

Soon after this dream I started asking Shereena to encourage me whenever she could. We also started rejoicing in the Lord together on purpose, every day.

This was around the same time we started working on this book. I knew for a while that I would be sharing my testimony, but I didn't know it would be in a book. A little while later as I was praying, God showed me that I could include Shereena's dreams in the book, to help illustrate what happened and bring character to the book without gossiping. That really brought me a lot of peace, because while I knew I had to tell my testimony to overcome the enemy, I didn't want to stir up strife with people. I wanted to focus on exposing our real enemy, the devil, and his principalities and demons.

A couple months earlier someone had prophesied to us that we would be doing ministry together as the Rhema and Logos combined... they were right!

It was also around this time that I got even further insight into Jezebel. For a long time I really didn't understand how godly ministers and artists could be affected by worldly business practices. Even as I noticed a barrage of Christian artists and ministers falling in sin, I really didn't know the root cause. I chalked it up to the normal struggle against sin, and maybe a lack of accountability and real Christian fellowship.

But by this time I had personally experienced the hypocrisy, cut-throat tactics, worldly business principles, adultery, slander, lying, and compromise in what I thought to be quality Christian ministry. My family and finances also had been severely affected by it.

Even after all this, I still wanted to promote the same artists, because they were preachers of the gospel. My thought was that "Nobody's perfect, we still have to keep trying to reach the world with the gospel." I still didn't understand what the root problem was.

One reason that it took so long for me to get a full revelation of Jezebel was because people that spoke against compromise in Christian music didn't really use scriptural authority. It's easy to see sin in secular music, or false doctrine, but it's much harder to discern error in spiritual things. I had heard plenty of people point the finger, use fallacious arguments, and preach their opinion about Christian music artists that they didn't like. But no one had really explained biblically how to distinguish between the holy and the profane. I appreciate the gifts of discerning of spirits, but when it comes to doctrine, there is really no authority to edify the Body of Christ by pointing the finger.

Personally, I didn't like when artists copied off of the world, but I didn't have any solid doctrine against it, so I tolerated it. My opinion was, I'd rather support the truth than fight the truth. So until that point, my doctrine on music was, "If the lyrics are scriptural, then the music is sanctified by the word and prayer." I had discussed and debated and defended this too, and no one had any teaching that could refute it. But one day I realized that most of the Christian artists that were spoken against for copying and partnering with the world had also since fallen in sin. There had to be something more to this.

I had also seen many people who were on fire for God and involved in Christian music completely fall away from the faith. I used to just chalk it up to compromise and the devil's deception, and I always preached against it, stood against it, and even lost friends for taking a stand against secular entertainment. But now I was beginning to see the source of the compromise and the stronghold of the deception even more clearly. It wasn't just in the world, it was in the Church.

As I was meditating and praying one morning, God revealed a new dimension of understanding on a scripture that I had studied, and even written about before. I already understood Jezebel as one who introduces compromise and idolatry into the church, but after meditating more and comparing it to what had happened in my life the past few years, I got an even deeper understanding of specifically how she did this. That morning God told me to look at Revelations 2 again. My whole doctrine on music was about to get adjusted, tweaked and improved.

## Scripture

### Addressing Jezebel's Stumbling Blocks

Jesus Christ is marching and he's chopping off heads. Everything that exalts itself above the knowledge of Christ is about to be dethroned (2 Corinthians 10:5). Just like Jehu, he's about to get rid of Jezebel. He's already been doing it, we just need to have an ear to hear and eyes to see what He's doing. Jezebel 1.0, the Old Covenant version of Jezebel, is the one that kills true messengers of God, and corrupts leaders. Jezebel 2.0, the New Covenant (after she killed John the Baptist and Jesus died and rose) version of Jezebel – her strategy is a little different:

> Revelations 2:18 And unto the angel of the church in Thyatira write; These things saith the Son of God, who hath his _eyes like unto a flame of fire_, and his

> *feet are like fine brass; 19 I know thy works, and charity, and service, and faith, and thy patience, and thy works; and the last to be more than the first. 20 Notwithstanding I have a few things against thee, because thou sufferest that woman Jezebel, which calleth herself a prophetess, to teach and to seduce my servants to commit fornication, and to eat things sacrificed unto idols.*

The Church in Thyatira was an awesome church – they had love, good works, and their works were continually growing. (See How to Get Authority over Nations - www.Sospression.com). However, when the Lord Jesus looked at them with His eyes as a flame of fire and feet like brass, he said He only had one thing against them – they tolerated Jezebel. Jezebel taught fornication (mixing with the world's ways) and idolatry (eating food that was sacrificed to idols, aka God's music that the devil has stolen).

When Jesus said that His eyes were like flames of fire, it meant He can see all, penetrate through all, and search the hidden thoughts and intents of the heart. When He said His feet were like brass, He was saying He has the authority to stand in His Church and be unmovable. As we focus on Christ, we can have those same eyes of fire that see through the world's lies. We can have beautiful bronze spiritual feet that are unmovable. We can know that we don't have to change or compromise to reach people with the gospel of peace.

Jezebel taught God's servants how to fornicate (mix with the world spiritually). She also taught them how to eat food sacrificed to idols. It's one thing to take back something that the devil has stolen, and sanctify it with the word and prayer. This is good. It's a completely different thing to teach God's servants that you have to copy from the world in order to be successful in ministry. This is bad. Let's look at a "chicken" example:

*Romans 14:13 Let us not therefore judge one another any more: but judge this rather, that <u>no man put a stumbling block or an occasion to fall in his brother's way.</u> 14 I know, and am <u>persuaded by the Lord Jesus, that there is nothing unclean of itself: but to him that esteemeth any thing to be unclean, to him it is unclean.</u>*

The same Lord Jesus that said that nothing is unclean of itself, is the same Lord Jesus that said He does not tolerate Jezebel teaching her servants to eat things sacrificed to idols. He does not tolerate stumbling blocks. How do we reconcile this? It will take some meditation and some spiritual understanding.

**How is Music Similar to Meat?**

Both music and meat are inanimate objects, created by God. Chicken is not bad in and of itself, it was only considered evil or good based on what it was sacrificed to. In the same way, a note, a sound, or a chord progression has no intrinsic evil in it. It's only considered evil or good based on what it is sacrificed to, or used for. Life and death are in the power of the tongue. Words are spirit and life. So the lyrics determine the sanctity of the music. So just as food is sanctified by the word and prayer, music is set apart for the purpose of the Word and the prayers that it's united with. So the words that come to your mind when you hear a certain musical piece determine what type of music it is.

Let's say there is a meat market called "Allah's Fowl Market." We know that all chicken is created by Jesus Christ, so "Allah's Fowl" really means nothing to us. We are free. So whatever chicken we eat, we can sanctify it with the Word and prayer, to the glory of God, and it will be alright (1 Timothy 4:4, 5).

But if we TEACH God's people to shop at Allah's Fowl Market; that the chicken there is better than all the other markets... and if you want to have a good meal, you gotta get it from Allah's Fowl Market, then serve it to God's people... you are setting a stumbling block before God's true servants (1 Corinthians 10:19-29).

1. While they shop at Allah's Fowl Market they will leave out with more than just chicken.
2. They will influence others to get their chicken from Allah's rather than their own farm.

I hope you get this little parable. When we teach people that they have to copy from the world to be successful in ministry, they will end up picking up sins (bad character) from the world too. They won't be able to distinguish between clean and unclean. That is why a lot of the most successful copycat artists in gospel music end up falling into sin. Not because they didn't sanctify their music with the word and prayer, but because while they were "shopping," they unknowingly picked up more than just music - wicked business practices, lust, pride, iniquity and other things. Then they end up doing in the natural the same things that they have been doing spiritually. They end up in adultery, and doing everything for more and more money, which is idolatry. Then their disciples - that they teach by example and who look up to them because they are successful - learn how to get their inspiration from the world as well, and they follow the same path. The cycle continues.

So whatever artistic style you had before you got saved, keep it. Change your message and use it for God (1 Corinthians 7:20). His words are spirit and life, they will change you.

But after you renew your mind - go hard into God's Spirit of Creativity, and stay unspotted from the World! Don't make excuses to go back to your old vomit. Don't go back to spiritual fornication and idolatry for your artistic inspiration. Your ministry will develop into something creative from God's Spirit and not an imitation of the world.

Remember, that Thyatira was not a bad church. Thyatira was actually a very good church, they were fruitful and productive, and they were actually growing in productivity. Jesus was pleased with the Church, they worked hard, they had love, service, faith... and their works kept

Esosa and Shereena Osai

growing. Jesus was pleased with everything except for a few things. The main thing wrong with them was their tolerance of Jezebel.

In the New Covenant, Jezebel 2.0 works in ministry. She called herself a prophetess. But her ministry methods are very off. Jezebel teaches God's servants to commit fornication (to mix with unbelievers in ministry, and adopt sinful characteristics from the world). She also teaches God's servants to eat food sacrificed to idols (consuming sin-inspired "soul" food – aka, publishing and entertainment that contains deception). She is tolerated by the Church, and they let her teach this and entice people to do it. What's the best way to teach? By example. What's the best way to seduce? To show off the benefits of sin.

> *Revelations 2:20 Notwithstanding I have a few things against thee, because thou sufferest that woman Jezebel, which <u>calleth herself a prophetess</u>, to teach and to seduce my servants to commit fornication , and to eat things sacrificed unto idols.*

## Eating with Demons, Sleeping with Demons, Produces Dead Children

If you get rid of your tolerance of Jezebel's compromise, worldliness, and idolatry, you will be blessed with great authority over nations.

> *Revelations 2:26 And he that overcometh, and keepeth my works unto the end, to him will I give power over the nations: 27 And he shall rule them with a rod of iron; as the vessels of a potter shall they be broken to shivers: even as I received of my Father. 28 And I will give him the morning star.*

But if you don't, there are tremendous judgments. There is tribulation for those who commit adultery with her, and her children will be killed with death. We think that what we are doing is okay, and that mixing with the world is a light thing, but Jesus calls Jezebel's doctrine "the depths of satan."

> *Revelations 2:21 And I gave her space to repent of her fornication; and she repented not. 22 Behold, <u>I will cast her into a bed, and them that commit adultery with her into great tribulation,</u> except they repent of their deeds. 23 <u>And I will kill her children with death</u>; and all the churches shall know that I am he which searcheth the reins and hearts: and I will give unto every one of you according to your works. 24 But unto you I say, and unto the rest in Thyatira, <u>as many as have not this doctrine, and which have not known the depths of Satan,</u> as they speak; I will put upon you none other burden.*

This is very serious. He gave her time to repent. But if she doesn't, she will get sick, those that commit adultery with her will go into great tribulation unless they repent. Her children (so-called spiritual fruit) will be killed with death. All the churches will know that Jesus is not playing and that His eyes are like fire, and they can't hide.

This is why artists that mix with the world and copy music from the world start off okay when they first get saved, but then they end up going through times of great trouble. And their spiritual children end up spiritually dead. It's only the artists and ministers that press past their initial inspiration and learn how to draw from God's Spirit that end up spiritually fruitful long term.

At the time of this writing, Jezebel is running rampant through the Church. People are dying, people are being exposed as adulterers, and there is divorce all over the church. We don't know that it's because Jesus is judging Jezebel, spiritually. The people that haven't fallen naturally yet have fallen spiritually, so it's just a matter of time before it manifests in the natural. And even if they don't "fall" publicly, they left God, so that's even worse.

Are you tired of seeing all the "top" gospel artists and big time preachers divorcing, committing adultery, partnering with unbelievers in ministry, copying and following secular artists, and copying ungodly business principles? The natural adultery and fornication only represents the spiritual adultery and fornication (1 Corinthians 15:46). But **even if** the spiritual sin doesn't fully manifest into natural fornication or natural divorce, **what's really worse?** Idolatry is spiritual fornication. Apostasy is divorce from God.

> **Apostasy:** (Greek) Apostasia, a falling away, defection, apostasy.
>
> *2 Thessalonians 2:3 Let no man deceive you by any means: for that day shall not come, except there come a falling away first, and that man of sin be revealed, the son of perdition;*
>
> **Divorce:** (Greek) Apostasion- divorce, repudiation, a bill of divorce

So "falling away" from God (apostasy) and "putting away" (divorce) are closely related. So now we have an insight into why there is so much divorce in the Church. Some of us have fallen away from God. The natural reflects the spiritual.

## Raising Our Standard and Eradicating Jezebel's Methods of Ministry

Ministries under Jezebel's influence teach Jezebel's doctrine by example. They say they do it to reach more people, but Jesus sees through that lie. It may be thru ignorance, but it is inspired by Jezebel for money and power. We need to repent and stop tolerating it. It more serious than we think, and it's spiritually satanic.

Now some religious hypocrites will read this and say: "See that's why I like that old school gospel music..." But did you know "that old school" was copied directly off of the world too? At its start, some gospel music was taken directly from the blues. (Here I'm not talking about Negro spirituals, I'm talking about Thomas Dorsey directly taking secular music, changing the lyrics and making them "gospel"). It's not about what "style" of music is bad or good; because God created all, and

Satan is incapable of creation. It's really about the direct source of inspiration for the piece. The question is: are the makers of gospel music still copycatting idolatry, or are they receiving inspiration from God?

Remember that "Nothing is unclean of itself, It's only he that esteems it unclean" (Romans 14:14). It's not that "Allah's Fowl Market" has evil chickens. What's wrong is when you teach people how to "shop" at "Allah's Fowl Market." You are teaching them how to stumble. Instead, teach people how to stay separate from worldly influences and to instead draw from the Spirit of God.

To put it plainly: if your first album sounds like the Christian version of your favorite unsaved artist, that's okay. You have space to repent. But if your second and third album still sounds like them, and you even change your sound to follow the sound of the most current sinful artists? Then you are probably under the compromising influence of Jezebel, and it's going to cost you severely, no matter how productive you think you are. Your lyrics could have all the scripture in the Bible, but if artistically you are feeding people a regurgitated version of idolatry, eventually they will find out your real source of inspiration.

There's nothing wrong with seeking to understand culture and language while you reach out to unbelievers one-on-one. I like to call music the "cultural conversation." There's nothing wrong with joining the "cultural conversation" and gaining influence for Christ. But there is something wrong with copycatting sin, and teaching God's servants to eat food sacrificed to idols. There is something wrong with partnering with unbelievers in business and teaching God's people to fornicate with the world. Jesus's **eyes like flames of fire** see the thoughts and intents of the heart, and He knows the difference.

Let me be clear: Satan does not create any musical notes or chords. He doesn't originate any drum beats, or vocal patterns. But if your "ministry" technique is to directly copy pieces that have been stolen by Satan, then you will end up being influenced by the wrong spirit. You and your disciples will suffer consequences.

*Revelations 2:21 And I gave her space to repent of her fornication; and she repented not. 22 Behold, I will <u>cast her into a bed, and them that commit adultery with her into great tribulation,</u> except they repent of their deeds.*

Drench your music and artistry so hard in the Word and Spirit of God that it is clear that it was born of God. In other words, do the same thing for your music that Christ did for you! That way, when people imitate you and seek your inspiration, they end up going towards the Spirit of God, not some sinful source.

What about the listener? As a listener, how can you tell if a Christian artist is a copycat, or being truly creative? The answer is: You can only judge what you know. If you don't know secular, then you won't recognize a copy. That's a good thing. The bible says to be ignorant concerning evil (Romans 16:19).

First, judge the lyrics. If they are scriptural, then it's okay. But if you find out somehow that they are copying certain songs from sinful sources, then be careful and do not tolerate it.

When it comes to promoting music and artists, I've learned to be even more careful than that. The Bible says to "lay hands on no man suddenly." Okay, so their music is scriptural. What about their lifestyle and character? Nobody is perfect, but get to know people personally. The Bible says "Know those that labor among you (1 Thessalonians 5:12)." What direction is their character leading them in? Get to know their source of inspiration, not just lyrically but musically. What direction are they going creatively? Are they still copying from the world, seeking to feed God's people food offered to idols? Or are they using their own God-given talents, diligence, and Holy Spirit creativity to express from heaven to today's culture?

So to the main points - what is important in music and ministry?

**Truth**: from the Word of God, not lies from Satan.

**Character:** from the Love of God, not worldly methods.

**Creativity**: from the Spirit of God, not pieces that have been knowingly sacrificed to idols.

Realize that this message is not condemnation or legalism – it is improvement, pruning, and purification. Thyatira was already a very good church, with growing works (Revelations 2:19). It's just that Jesus sees more, He wants more, He demands more, and He rewards more.

**Let me repeat that. This is not condemnation, this is purification. Jesus sees more, Jesus wants more, Jesus demands more, and Jesus will reward more.**

Every genre of Kingdom music goes through phases. First there's the phase of getting biblical lyrically. Then there's the phase of getting a standard of quality. Then there's the phase of getting originality and creativity from God. Then God really starts getting the glory! It's time for a new phase in Kingdom music. Now that we have scriptural ammunition, let's prune ourselves to bear more fruit for the Kingdom of God!

**What about Paul when he said I become all things to all men that I may win some?**

What does this look like? Does this look like going among people, talking to them, reaching out to them for real, and learning their language? Or does this look like being a copycat or an actor? There's nothing wrong with finding out a language or a musical style that people speak, and speaking the same language they speak to win them. Just be original, be inspired by God, and don't take the lazy copycat route. You give more glory to God when you can make it obvious that God is your source. Give a fresh take in every way.

If I'm a missionary and I go learn another culture's language, I can get respect and win them. If I go and try to impersonate their chief, they just think I'm a comedian. If I go and I mix my religious beliefs with theirs, then they won me - I haven't won them. If I go to the local witch doctor and mix my religion with his, seeking to use his influence, then they won me, I haven't won them.

## Didn't Paul quote a secular poet?

What Paul used wasn't sinful. He quoted a line from a poem that was harmless, and actually was true and verifiable by scripture. He also was clear that this was "your" poet. Showing separation, "your source is not mine." His ministry was original. Paul was not afraid to show holiness (Acts 17:28). That would be like a Christian rapper saying "your rapper said this." But the Christian rapper has a completely original sound, and is not trying to be a carbon copy of the secular rapper or partner with them in ministry.

## Hypothetical Question #1 for Jezebel – How do you affect the next generation of musicians?

If I'm a young aspiring singer or artist, and I see that all of the top Christian singers and artists all imitate and partner with secular artists... what do you think I will do? I will **listen to and follow secular artists for inspiration** for my ministry. I will think I have arrived when I finally get enough respect from sinners to partner with them and make money with them, and use **their influence** to mix our messages.

I have seen young Christian artists and musicians with talent and originality be discouraged, led astray, or totally fall away after they realize that the Christian artists that they look up to are really following secular artists. God takes them to a new place of originality and creativity, but they are scared to go there because they don't think they will reach as many people or make as much money for their family as the copycat artists and mixture musicians do. They trip over the stumbling-block.

*Revelations 2:20 Notwithstanding I have a few things against thee, because thou sufferest that woman Jezebel, which calleth herself a prophetess, <u>to teach</u>*

*and to seduce my servants to commit fornication ,
and to eat things sacrificed unto idols.*

### Hypothetical Question #2 for Jezebel – What Example Do You Give to Youth?

If we are instructing our youth to be holy and separate from the world, by being careful what music they listen too... and then the biggest Christian artists that we promote are carbon copies of secular artists, what is that saying to our youth?

It's pretty much showing them that we are not holy, we are just followers. So why would they follow us when they can go directly to the world? Then they leave us, go to the world and they die spiritually.

I have seen this happen time and time again. I'm not saying that if the world uses a guitar, we can't use a guitar. Or if the world uses drums, we can't use drums. What I'm saying is that there is a spiritual, lyrical, musical, and artistic **source of inspiration** that should be completely holy. The remixes, the copycat voices, and the secular partnerships may generate attention; but they have long term negative effects that you don't expect.

> *Revelations 2:23 And I will kill her children with death; and all the churches shall know that I am he which searcheth the reins and hearts: and I will give unto every one of you according to your works.*

**But if I don't copy off of the world or partner with sinners, my music, my ministry, my business won't be as good as what the world has, and it won't reach enough people?**

When you commit spiritual fornication, or feed God's people food that has been sacrificed to idols, you are not "reaching" anybody. This is a mask for **covetousness**, or for **pre-eminence**. You may desire to make more money. You may want a higher level of influence - from the wrong source - so you can be honored by other men. You don't want to take up your cross and you don't believe that God has the power to help you reach people through His holiness and His Holy Spirit creativity and originality.

**But I need to follow secular artists because they are the best at their craft, and I need to improve. I just like them a lot, I'm tired of hearing wack Christians!**

Well, if you really understood your craft you would be able to hone your own voice and style. People that understand lyricism and poetic meter can write in their own voice. People that really know music can differentiate a melody or a rhythm. If the Creator is the Source of Creativity, and you are plugged into Him, then you have access to a new song. You have time to repent. You have no excuse to imitate.

If I happen to be riding down the street or walking in a mall, and - with my musical ear - I hear some music or lyrical patterns that sound nice, I can notice it but I won't give my soul to it unless I agree with it. And if I make music I don't need to copy it. If I really get the craft of it I can make my own sound completely unique. I can be a leader, not a follower, especially if <u>I don't want to give them the glory that God deserves.</u>

### Hypothetical Question #3 for Jezebel – Are You Cutting God's Glory in Half?

I remember once I really liked this Christian worship band. Their focus on Jesus was awesome, their hunger for God was awesome, and their lyrics were scriptural and prophetic. I bought many of their albums. Maybe a year or so afterwards, I ran across some information online about them, and found out their sound was considered a copy of U2.

I had never heard any U2 songs. So when it comes to how the music affected me, it didn't remind me of any U2 songs, so I didn't stumble when I listened to it. But when I found out their musical **inspiration,** I was somewhat disappointed. Previously, I was able to give God 100% of the glory for this Christian band. But now, I could only give God glory for their lyrics. Their musical sound was considered a carbon copy of a secular band. So in my mind, God's glory was practically cut in half. It cut my excitement and made me feel like a follower.

Think about it – does God lack creativity? No, He is the Creator. Can Christian musicians develop new sounds? Yes. Why do they choose not to? Even in our Christian bookstores, they advertise: "If you like _____ secular artist, then you will love _____ Christian artist." This is a shame and an affront to God's glorious creativity, leadership, and originality. I can't wait for the day when Christians are leaders in creativity and originality from a place of holiness, instead of following unbelievers.

One of the ways this will happen is that we will begin to have faith in the creativity and inspiration of God. One of the awesome characteristics about anything inspired by God is that whatsoever is born of God has within it the power to overcome the world. It will overcome all the hindrances and roadblocks that Satan will set up against it. This faith will give us victory that overcomes.

## VICTORY OVERCOMES

Jesus Christ is God and King, and obedience to His commandments brings you Victory over the world, since He is the King of the World. But since He is currently waiting for His enemies to be made His footstool, it takes faith to make this victory happen.

> *1 John 5:4 For whatsoever is born of God overcometh the world: and this is the victory that overcometh the world, even our faith.*

Let's separate two elements of this scripture:

1. Whatever is born of God overcomes the world.
2. The victory that overcomes the world is our faith.

First you get victory through faith. Then, **that victory overcomes the world by faith**. Where does that faith come from? It's born from God.

Let's resynthesize the elements of this scripture:

Whatever faith, belief, vision, confession, saying, profession, ministry, obedient action, message... that is born from, conceived from, originated from God the Father in Heaven... **IS the VICTORY** that is designed to overcome, conquer, and gain supremacy over... the world's system, the world's ways, the world's sinful methods and strategies that originated in Satan, sin, and the prince of this world.

The faith that GOD gave you will always overcome the sinful ways and methods of the world. It's a guarantee! But you must *actively believe and confess it*, and it must be *born and originated from God*.

"God I thank you for an original faith and vision given from you, not from my own mind or Satan! I will continue to work the faith in Christ that you have given me, and watch it overcome the sinful ways of the world."

Let the true sons of the kingdom of God arise! Our ministries, our music, our business practices, our messages, all originate from God, and are guaranteed to overcome the world! But we have to believe in God more than we believe in the world.

## Interpretation

The woman was another incarnation of Jezebel. She was trying to destroy my wife and I with depression and suicidal thoughts. She was accepted in the church, just as she was in the Revelations 2 church of Thyatira. She called herself a prophetess.

Even though I hated secular music and secular entertainment. I still ignorantly tolerated Jezebel. I did this by allowing ministers whose method of "ministry" was to copy a song or style from the world, change the lyrics, and feed it to God's people. Not all of the music was Jezebellic, but some was. When people that knew secular music told me about it, I didn't respond rightly. I tolerated it because the lyrics were scriptural. That gave Jezebel entrance into our life, especially when she got angry with me for exposing her secular servants.

This understanding also helped me understand all the earlier dreams of adultery. Some of the artists that I worked with were scripturally solid, but artistically compromising. They copied secular artists, and people knew it. The dreams that my wife had of me in bed with other women were partly a representation of the spirit of Jezebel's fornication.

When God gave me further understanding of Jezebel in this form, my wife and I were able to use our weapons and cut her head off. We conquered depression by confessing and professing our faith daily, and rejoicing daily. We are doing this now on a larger scale with the word of our testimony, and by adjusting our ministry to our increased understanding. We seek to inspire artists to be creative, not copycats from the world. We also check into the source of inspiration and lifestyle before we promote an artist, even if their music is scripturally sound.

## Application

**Get to the root of Jezebel's Influence in the Church, and chop her head off.**

Don't tolerate idolatry, covetousness, greed, or spiritual fornication in yourself.

**Don't tolerate "ministry" strategies that include idolatry and spiritual mixture with sinful ways, or copycatting sin, or business and ministry partnerships with unbelievers.**

If you are bearing fruit in ministry, and experience difficulties, don't let discouragement set in. Just know that you are being pruned and purified so that you can bear even more fruit (John 15). Just be open to God's voice.

Require any minister in God's church to declare their source of inspiration, and prove they are not just copying the world's system: musically, message-wise, or business wise.

It's sad that many artists and ministers would rather partner with or imitate a sinful minister than publicly call them to repentance. Don't be a political Ahab or idolatrous Jezebel - be Elijah, and support Elijah's that are bold and unafraid to expose idolatry.

Know those that labor among you.

**Realize that the Scriptures and God's Spirit of Creativity are an endless source of inspiration** and wisdom, there is no need for another.

**Realize that spiritual adultery is not the means of evangelism.** Jesus ate with sinners because they wanted to repent in response to His preaching and His compassion, not because He needed their influence. Holiness is the ground floor of all effective ministry fruit that remains long term.

**Realize that spiritual fornication and adultery leads to physical fornication and adultery.** Be separate and holy.

BELIEVE THAT WHATEVER IS BORN OF GOD HAS VICTORY OVER THE WORLD! Don't settle for anything less. Believe God for His Glory to be Revealed!

**When God's Musicians and Singers and Songwriters get their Creativity from God and from diligence in their talents, and in worship & prayer meetings - instead of copycatting from secular radio and videos, the Church will be led into Holiness, and We Will SEE the LORD!**

# 9

# REPENTANCE: TURNING OUR HEARTS BACK TO GOD

**Enemy Profile:** Us. You and Me. We are the ones that God left in charge, so it's all our fault! Everyone has a Right to Repent!

**Shereena's Dream**

*The Cry : October 2011*

*We had an auditorium in a high school to have meetings about The Call Detroit. We would cycle groups of people in and give a presentation to each group and have prayer and worship... There were points when I would be upfront speaking, telling the people about The Call, and they would just sit waiting to be entertained. Group after group would come in and would have the same blank look.*

*Then a group of high school students were coming into the auditorium to hear The Call presentation. As they were filing into the auditorium I overheard a male student telling a smaller male student that he was going to sodomize him at this meeting. He said "I just want a date", date was the code word for sodomy. When I heard that I ran to tell Lou and the Elders who were strategizing in the foyer. When I told them, the Elders ran in with haste (All older white men). I followed them in but by the time we got back in there (which took about 60 seconds) the offense had already happened. The meeting was canceled due to the offense and the students were already cleared out of the room. A custodian was mopping up the blood in the small, open bathroom off of the auditorium where the offense had taken place. When I saw that it was too late and realized the sadness of what just happened, I began to weep and cry aloud very bitterly. Another adult group came in and I began to scream over the microphone, cry out to the Lord, we have to cry out! And some older black men began to sing on the microphone as the band played. I started telling the group why The Call was coming and about the terrible things going on in this city, but I did not have any official statistics, only the example of what just happened with the high school students. Even though I was crying and screaming for people to cry out to the Lord, they gave little or no response... The victim and the aggressor in the offense were both very broken. When the high school students came in a very evil presence had filled the place. They had no knowledge of the things of God. It was as if they were being raise by evil.*

### Real Life

During the time when we had first officially started the Detroit Area House of Prayer, I can remember God crying through me twice. I say God crying through me, because that's how it felt – it was extreme, and it was powerful. My personality is very reserved, and usually non-emotional. I don't really cry a lot, and I'm not an actor; so I took note that this was the Holy Ghost.

The second time it happened, I was substitute teaching in a high school. It was like I was in a scripted movie. It was like God was highlighting certain voices in the room. I started to notice that the same students that talked about how they went to church were the ones with the foulest mouths. I started to hear students talk about how they were going to have sex on prom night. Then I was reading the Detroit Free Press website. That day the site did a story on a local church, and their choir was singing on a video on the site. I looked closely, and could not believe my eyes! One of the same students that had just sat in front of me planning his prom night exploits was singing in the choir on the video!

That whole day, it got progressively worse and worse. I don't even remember some of the things I heard, and I don't want to! For some reason, that day God was showing me specifically the church kids that were off the hook. I was praying for the kids, and saying as much as I could. On the way to my car after the day was over, I felt the tears start to flow. I actually rushed to my car because it felt uncontrollable, and I didn't want anyone to see me. When I opened my car my heart broke, the tears burst out, and it wasn't just tears, it was full-fledged wailing. The Holy Spirit was crying through me. It continued, I called my wife to talk and she couldn't even understand what I was saying.

That summer we continued to pray. God continued to show us wisdom and revelation, especially confirming His blueprint for our lives. We realized that some of the things we had experienced since we were married were God showing us the principalities and strongholds that held back the Harvest in the Church.

We had known for almost a year that we were going to have to tell our testimony to get victory over Satan, but we had no idea it was going to be a book. When I finally got the key of revelation - on who Jezebel really was - all of the dreams of the past 3 years were unlocked. Instantly we knew it was God writing a story, and it was going to be a book. God dropped the blueprint, and we wrote 90% of this book in about 2 weeks. The grace of God was on us to do it.

In our personal lives, we realized that Jezebel had been loosed against us because we fought with her 1.0 version at the same time that we tolerated her 2.0 version through promoting copycat Christian music, such as remixes and secular imitators. We realized that Judas had been loosed against us because we used birth control for almost the whole first year of our marriage. We didn't realize that taking control of when

God gave us children based on our own understanding was rooted in pragmatism.

We were glad that God showed us and allowed us to have the conflict that took us higher. This was better than continuing in ignorance, or blindly submitting to Satan while trying to do God's work. We ended up repenting for everything we did, and even some things we didn't do!

Wisdom and revelation continued to flow in abundance. God gave us a lot more vision and strategy for turning the hearts of the generation back to God.

That fall was a season of transition. We ended up volunteering with Lou Engle and the The Call for The Call Detroit 11.11.11. Lou Engle is a man who has been laboring for over 20 years in prayer, preaching, writing, and hosting solemn assemblies to turn America back to God. He calls elders, young people, and the whole generation to repentance and prayer, and a Nazarite fasted lifestyle. It was such a pleasure to work with Lou and his team.

After we finished our testimony, things got much easier. I was able to find part-time employment to hold us over while still working to build the House of Prayer and work with The Call. The first week of the 40 day fast with The Call Strike Team, we found out we were pregnant again!

We still had trouble with a few things, but since we had revelation on the spiritual issues behind the scenes, we were able to deal with it more quickly and effectively. We ended up doing a series of prayer events leading up to The Call called iRepent. These events were to repent of specific principalities and strongholds that God showed us were in operation in the Body of Christ, and had to be repented of.

### Scripture

The Church has all authority in heaven and earth. We have authority to bind and loose. What we bind on earth will be bound in the atmosphere, and what we loose on earth will be loosed in the atmosphere, where angels and principalities war (Matthew 18:18). God has shown us that the root of many of the problems in our cities and nation are not because of sin outside the Church, but our toleration of sin **inside** the Church.

## WE ALREADY HAVE ALL THE AUTHORITY

The Authority of the Believer. We really have it! We are already on top. In Matthew 16 Jesus gave Peter the keys to the Kingdom of Heaven. He said:

> *Matthew 16:18 And I tell you that you are Peter, and on this rock I will build my church, and the gates of Hades will not overcome it. 19 I will <u>give you the keys of the kingdom of heaven</u>; whatever you bind on earth will be bound in heaven, and whatever you loose on earth will be loosed in heaven."*

We are not trying to get authority, we already have authority. The question becomes: **What are we doing with our authority**? What has the church been allowing (loosing) on earth, which has now been loosed in heaven (the atmosphere over the earth)? What has the church refused to tolerate (binding) that subsequently has been bound in heaven (the atmosphere over the earth)?

What we say goes - even if we don't quite understand it. What we tolerate gets spiritual power. What we don't tolerate loses spiritual power. If we as the Church want to change our cities and regions, it all starts with us. So many times we look up to government, media, entertainment, etc, when we should be looking down. Not looking down out of pride or because we are better than anyone else. We look down with our perspective, only because **Jesus put us on top.** We need to lift these areas up, because we are seated in heavenly places in Christ Jesus (Ephesians 1).

So many times, we point the finger of blame at unbelievers, when it's entirely our fault. Our frustration should not be with unbelievers, but our frustration should be with ourselves for giving unbelievers power to do what they do. My wife says all the time "If Christians didn't support wickedness, wickedness would fail." If everyone who claimed to be a Christian also stopped supporting wicked entertainment, then wicked entertainment would not be successful. I was guilty of this myself as a teenager.

**What if the solution to our city violence problems was Unity in the Church instead of the wars of words?**

**What if the solution to abortion was us accepting all the Children the Lord gave us instead of buying the lie that children are a loss instead of a profit?** I was guilty of this myself in the first few months of my marriage, using contraception instead of letting the Lord control and plan our family.

**What if the solution to protecting marriage was the Church protecting our marriages, and stopping the spiritual adultery that looses the physical adultery?**

**What if the solution to cultural pollution was purifying the worship in our own Churches, rebuilding the Tabernacle of David and keeping God's Levites employed in that work day and night?**

**What if the solution to racism was desegregating the Body of Christ and building a house of prayer for every ethnic group?**

### Obedience Fulfilled in the Church

When your obedience is fulfilled, I will revenge all disobedience (2 Corinthians 10). Judgment begins in the house of God (1 Peter 4). We ALREADY have the authority; we have just been using it all wrong. We need to REPENT and turn our hearts to God. What we bind is bound, and what we loose is loosed. **If it's bound, then we bound it. If it's loosed, then we loosed it.** We need to purify the Bride of Christ so that she can bind the wrong things and loose the right things in the Body of Christ, on earth. THEN it will be bound and loosed in the atmospheres over our cities.

*But where does the Word say that Christ's followers "already have ALL authority?" Only Christ has authority.*

Luke 10:19 - power to tread on the power of enemy (I GIVE YOU)

Matthew 16:19 - keys to the Kingdom of heaven (I GIVE YOU)

I believe that I GIVE YOU means that I give YOU. Peter and the disciples were the Church. I believe that that power, and those keys are still in the Church, collectively.

In Matthew 28:19, Jesus said that All power is given unto Me... therefore YOU go... Why would He tell US to do something with the power that HE has? Because we are in Him, of course. The Body of Christ collectively. This makes total sense, especially combined with Matthew 16:19 and Luke 10:19.

My goal is NOT to say that as individuals we have all power over heaven and earth. It's only in Christ as a whole Body.

*But doesn't God's Word say that it is GOD who controls, sets up, and takes down the authorities of this world?*

Yes this is true, but God also gives authority to humans, and what we do with it matters. If we disobey him, there are consequences. There are even many examples in the Bible where God anoints wicked leaders to chastise His people for their sins. When His people repent, God gives them better leaders.

We need to know that, as Christians, what we do actually matters, because we are in Christ, and He has authority in Heaven and earth. Our actions have greater consequences.

*But I thought we were just supposed to preach and minister the Gospel to individuals and make disciples of Christ. Why are you talking about authority and worldly government?*

Our authority is spiritual. Yes, we do preach the gospel to individuals. But God anointed Paul to preach to "kings" as well. He went to the political leaders of many cities, even the barbarian island. That's the new testament. Our job is not just to preach the gospel of individual salvation, but the gospel of the Kingdom (Matt 24). Jesus is King of all, coming back to literally reign. Everything must adjust to His truth. We don't need government positions to do this, but we do proclaim all truth. Everyone has a right to repent, no matter if their job is sweeping floors, or making laws. This repentance also has "fruits of repentance" (Matthew 3:8).

I am not saying that there will be a utopia in our cities if Christians get it together. That will not come until Jesus literally and physically returns to earth. But we can make a much **bigger difference.** There can be a much **bigger difference** between us and the world. When God delivered Moses from Egypt (Exodus), none of the plagues that were on the Egyptians touched the land of Goshen. Why? Because God heard the Cry of His people who desired nothing but the freedom from oppression and the freedom to worship Him.

## Mark the Ones Who Cry

*Ezekiel 9 ³And the glory of the God of Israel was gone up from the cherub, whereupon he was, to the threshold of the house. And he called to the man clothed with linen, which had the writer's inkhorn by his side; ⁴And <u>the LORD said unto him, Go through the midst of the city, through the midst of Jerusalem,</u>* ***<u>and set a mark upon the foreheads of the men that sigh and that cry for all the abominations</u>*** *<u>that be done in the midst thereof.</u> ⁵And to the others he said in mine hearing, Go ye after him through the city, and smite: let not your eye spare, neither have ye pity:* ***⁶<u>Slay utterly old and young</u>***<u>, both maids, and little children, and women:</u> ***but come not near any man upon whom is the mark; and begin at my sanctuary.*** *Then they began at the ancient men which were before the house.*

Where are those in God's house who will cry out? Who will literally cry for the abominations done in His sanctuary? For the unclean being called clean? The church celebrates while "gospel" singers and choirs sing with worldly purposes. Who is going to cry out about homosexuality being tolerated in the church? About the fornication that is tolerated and covered up for in the church? About the children who are neglected and left to the school system and entertainment? Where is the CRY?!

We as the body of Christ must be sensitive to the heart of God. We must love what He loves and hate what He hates. In Ezekiel 9 those who were troubled by the ungodliness going on in God's house, those who cried about it, who lamented over it, who hurt over it - these were sealed from destruction. Why? They took the time to seek and know God. They loved God's commands and hated the ways of the flesh. Those who knew of the abominations, who saw the evil happening in God's temple, but who did not cry, who were indifferent, who pretended not to see, not to know - they were given over to destruction. Where are those who CRY?!

Our young people are being taken from the church to the world, and into hell, before our eyes... **WHERE IS THE CRY?!**

Our marriage covenants are being broken, God hates divorce... **WHERE IS THE CRY?!**

Pastors are preaching and teaching false doctrine and we eat it... **WHERE IS THE CRY?!**

Fasting and prayer and studying God's word is the ONLY way to have your eyes open to the truth, to know God's heart, to understand the seriousness of the hour. According to Psalms 19, in order to see our sin, we must know and treasure God's law, testimonies, statutes, commandment, fear of God, and God's judgments. Then we will see our errors, and be cleansed from secret faults, and sin will not have dominion over us. (See Appendix A – Spirituals and Naturals on Fasting.)

**Prayer, Fasting, and Repentance Preaching**

Our faith is the victory that overcomes the world, but we also need prayer, fasting and repentance. We need to repent and turn our hearts back to God!

> *Matthew 17: 20 If ye have faith as a grain of mustard seed, ye shall say unto this mountain, Remove hence to yonder place; and it shall remove; and nothing shall be impossible unto you. 21 Howbeit this kind goeth not out but by prayer and fasting.*

The key to turning a nation is in God's people turning our hearts back to God. Sometimes we aren't even aware of the sins that we have committed. We think that how we live and what we do as the Church is normal and Godly.

## We Need a Messenger

**A messenger of God, who will boldly and gently point out the specific sins and errors that we don't yet recognize is a crucial component of any revival and spiritual awakening that God seeks to bring to a people.**

> *2 Chronicles 7:14 If my people, which are called by my name, shall humble themselves, and pray, and seek my face, and turn from their wicked ways; then will I hear from heaven, and will forgive their sin, and will heal their land.*

We know this scripture back and forth, but what is missing? We have gatherings that are everything but solemn, and we have a Church culture that glosses over and covers up sins, rather than exposing them so that we can cry or **feel any Godly sorrow or emotion over them.** This stops us from turning to God from the heart, some only turn to God on the surface. God is going to turn this type of Church culture on its head. **God will send a messenger that will point out those things that we are currently unaware of**, and call us to repent.

**Repent:**
1. to change one's mind, i.e. to repent
2. to change one's mind for better, heartily to amend with abhorrence of one's past sins

## When Does the Joy Come?

*Luke 15:7 I say unto you, that likewise joy shall be in heaven over one sinner that repenteth, more than over ninety and nine just persons, which need \*no repentance.*

Is there anyone in the Church who is perfect, and "needs no repentance?" We are righteous by the blood of Christ, but when we really seek God and observe His ways, oftentimes we will find items where we **need repentance.** GOD in heaven has joy when those who have sinned repent and turn their heart to God.

We need to take part in the full emotion and personality of God. Full joy, full celebration, partying, music and dancing (Luke 15), but ONLY after we receive full vision, full disgust, crying and sadness over sin, and turning. No, its not bipolar disorder, or schizophrenia. It's abandoning our soul to Him and being filled with the Word and Spirit of God.

## iRepent

Daniel is an example of a man who turned a nation repenting and praying all by himself! He saw what was happening according to scripture. He responded in fasting, prayer, sackcloth and ashes. God responded by sending Him one of the highest ranking angels. God used His response of faith and humility to get His will done on earth. He also revealed to Daniel even more mysteries further down the line of history. Read Daniel 9.

**Daniel got deep revelation of scripture.** - Daniel responded to the Word of God with fear and trembling. He dove so deep into it that he realized it was time for its fulfillment. Then He responded with full knowledge of the seriousness of what Israel had done, knowing all the sins they have committed and how serious they were. He didn't gloss over anything, because He understood the book of Jeremiah and the Torah.

**Daniel knew His role. – Daniel understood the God/Man partnership.** God is Sovereign and Man has been given Authority. He knew He was responsible to pray into the will of God. He knew God presented His word not just to be heard, but to be interacted with, and engaged in, and acted upon, and enforced.

**Daniel repented by himself!** – One man turned a nation by repentance, prayer, sackcloth, and ashes. What can you do by yourself to turn your city or nation to God? You can have the highest ranking angels fighting principalities for God's will or trumpeting a supernatural message in response to your words!

**Daniel repented for things he didn't even do.** – Daniel repented on behalf of his whole nation and took responsibility. Oftentimes it's our little sins that allow the world to release big sins against us. We give the devil an inch in us, and that gives him a mile in the culture, and he can send his enemies after you according to what you did. But you can even turn your heart to God concerning the things you didn't do. You can sigh and cry and fast and pray for any abominations done, and God will respond and reward you.

**Daniel repented physically as well as spiritually.** – Daniel understood the principle "First the Natural, then the Spiritual." He didn't just pray it and say it. It got deep in his mind, and then it changed his emotions as well. Then he changed his clothes from fancy clothes to rags (sackcloth). He put dust on his face (ashes). He stopped eating pleasant food, choosing to avoid meats, sweets, and maybe even bread (Daniel 11 fast). Maybe he only ate raw food for a time (Daniel 1 fast). He may have even gone all-water for a couple of days (water fast). He got physical with his turning to God. (In the New Covenant we don't change our faces or clothing to fast, we fast in secret (Matthew 6)).

**God responded with power, authority, affection and revelation.** – **Power** – The nation was set in its path to fulfill Jeremiah's prophecy and return to Jerusalem. **Authority** – one of the highest ranking angels, Gabriel came to Him personally. **Affection** – He was called beloved of God. **Revelation** – he ended up with further knowledge of God's mystery and plan.

## Spiritual Violence is the Ground Floor of the Kingdom of God

> *Matthew 11:11 Verily I say unto you, Among them that are born of women there hath not risen a greater than John the Baptist: notwithstanding he that is least in the kingdom of heaven is greater than he. 12 And from the days of John the Baptist until now the kingdom of heaven suffereth violence , and the violent take it by force .*

Fasting, Prayer, and Preaching Repentance is Spiritual Violence. It's the Nazirite/Forerunner/Holiness anointing of John the Baptist that leads to the Kingdom. **Spiritual Violence is the Ground floor of the Kingdom of God**. And the least in the Kingdom of Jesus Christ is even greater than John the Baptist, because Jesus takes us higher. But even Jesus Christ Himself built from the ground floor of Spiritual Violence - fasting, prayer, and preaching repentance. Simple faith in the Blood and Cross of Christ gives you salvation. But kingdom dominion comes through spiritual violence.

> *Matthew 11:13 For all the prophets and the law prophesied until John. 14 And if ye will receive it, this is Elias, which was for to come . 15 He that hath ears to hear, let him hear. 16 But whereunto shall I liken this generation? It is like unto children sitting in the markets, and calling unto their fellows, 17 And saying, We have piped unto you, and ye have not danced; we have mourned unto you, and ye have not lamented. 18 For John came neither eating nor drinking, and they say, He hath a devil. 19 The Son of man came eating and drinking, and they say, Behold a man gluttonous, and a winebibber, a friend of*

*publicans and sinners. But wisdom is justified of her children.*

Haters are going to hate. Hard hearts don't move. If you sing a happy song they don't dance. If you sing a sad song they don't cry. If you fast and pray, and preach and live holiness - they call you extreme, crazy, "holier than thou." If you fast for 40 days, and then eat and drink - while you preach, teach and heal people, and fellowship with music and dancing – they say you are just a sinner.

But guess what? Obedience Works. Look at the Fruit!

Spiritual Authority. Spiritual Violence. God is POWERFUL when we are obedient. We obey in Humility and Self-Sacrifice, so God gets all the Glory.

## Jesus Christ Ministry Techniques

Some of God's people nowadays have really good intentions, but are mistakenly trying to be smarter than God. We've also got a lot of compromise and covetousness in "ministry". We have people singing and preaching a compromised message. As a result of the compromised message they end up committing spiritual adultery with the world and practicing idolatry.

What was Jesus' first message?

> *Mark 1:14: Now after that John was put in prison [the spirit of Ahab and Jezebel HATES the spirit of John the Baptist/Elijah], Jesus came into Galilee, preaching the gospel of the kingdom of God,* 15: *And saying,* **The time is fulfilled, and the kingdom of God is at hand: repent ye, and believe the gospel.**

Let's look at the specifics of Jesus' message:

1. **Time is fulfilled** – Urgency, time awareness

2. **Kingdom of God is here**. – New level of Authority is here

3. **Repen**t – Turn, change your mind and ways. Implying that what you are doing now is wrong

4. **Believe good news** – The Truth is good news and will leave you better off than you are now

Look at the record of His first message in the book of Matthew:

> *Matthew 1:17 From that time Jesus BEGAN to preach and to say Repent, for the Kingdom of Heaven is at hand.*

Did Jesus say, let me heal everybody first and build my relationships before I ease in the repentance message maybe sometime later? – **NO.**

Did Jesus try to attract as many people as possible with a positive and non-confrontational message, and then bring conviction and repentance into the picture afterwards? – **NO.**

Did Jesus try to get as many fans as possible first, or try to gain influence through relationships with influential sinners... and then bring the hard message of repentance in slowly after his platform was already set? – **NO.**

Jesus **BEGAN** His ministry message with repentance. Repentance means turn from what you are doing now, implying that what you are doing now is wrong. That brings a feeling of guilt and conviction.

Did Jesus have love? **Yes.**

Did Jesus show love to all? **Yes.**

Did Jesus heal people and cast out demons and do miracles? **Yes.**

Did Jesus meet people's natural and physical and emotional needs? **Yes.**

Did Jesus hide the truth and save the hard message of repentance until later – after he had done everything else first? – **NO.**

Actually, it was reversed. Jesus did the healing and relationship-building after people knew what He stood for and pointedly preached. He preached repentance from sin and the Kingdom of God. Most of the people who came to Him were **already humbled** by the message of repentance.

People love to acknowledge that Jesus ate with sinners, but let's also acknowledge that those sinners *were repenting* due to the message that Jesus was actually preaching. I'm not saying you have to clean yourself up before you come to Christ. I am saying there is a humility that you take when coming before God. There always has, and there always will be. God **only** hangs with humble people (James 5, 1 Peter 5). That's why preaching repentance is primary, if you really want people to be able to get through to God, not just you.

When Jesus preached, the only non-repentant people were the Pharisees. They had their own religious beliefs that prevented them from feeling the need to repent. They came to attack Jesus, and they got attacked back with Truth.

The people that fight the message of repentance (change towards God) and holiness – Gods purpose in everything – are normally the people who are comfortable in their very own personally invested religious tradition.

Let's look again at the forerunner of Jesus, John the Baptist. This was the prophet called to introduce people to Jesus. What did he preach?

### uRepent too!

> *Luke 3 ...the word of God came unto John the son of Zacharias in the wilderness. 3: And he came into all the country about Jordan, preaching **the baptism of repentance for the remission of sins**...Then said he to the multitude that came forth to be baptized of him,*

*O generation of vipers, who hath warned you to flee from the wrath to come?...*

*8: **Bring forth therefore fruits worthy of repentance**, and begin not to say within yourselves, We have Abraham to our father: for I say unto you, That God is able of these stones to raise up children unto Abraham.*

*9: And now also the axe is laid unto the root of the trees: every tree therefore which bringeth not forth good fruit is hewn down, and cast into the fire. 10: And the people asked him, saying, What shall we do then? 11: He answereth and saith unto them, He that hath two coats, let him impart to him that hath none; and he that hath meat, let him do likewise. 12: Then came also publicans to be baptized, and said unto him, Master, what shall we do? 13: And he said unto them, <u>Exact no more than that which is appointed you.</u>14: And the soldiers likewise demanded of him, saying, And what shall we do? And he said unto them, <u>Do violence to no man</u>, <u>neither accuse any falsely</u>; and be <u>content with your wages.</u>*

John the Baptist preached the baptism of repentance for the remission of sins (**Cancer that is in remission is not active**). He demanded proof and results of repentance. Not only was John direct, he was also specific and bossy! He told regular **people**, **government tax collectors**, and **government soldiers** exactly what to do with their <u>life and their financial resources.</u>

Let's go back to Jesus... From whom did Jesus get most of his initial disciples? They were initially followers of John the Baptist, who had repented with John's Baptism of Repentance. John the Baptist prepared many people to receive Jesus Christ by preaching repentance.

Most of the people that rejected John's message also rejected Jesus. Most of the people that received John's message also ended up receiving Jesus' message; even way later after Jesus died and rose again (See Acts 19:3-5, Acts 18:25). So how people respond to the message of repentance is a clue to how they will eventually respond to Jesus.

Don't let anyone tell you that you can't preach holiness or repentance, that all you can do is build relationships and hope that people will maybe sometime repent later. You don't have to be mean, but you do have to be clear. Relationship evangelism is good, but you don't have to hide holiness and repentance.

> Jude 1:21: *Keep yourselves in the love of God, looking for the mercy of our Lord Jesus Christ unto eternal life.*
> 22: *And of some have compassion, making a difference:*
> 23: *And others save with fear, pulling them out of the fire; hating even the garment spotted by the flesh.*

On some have compassion - save some with fear and hatred. (Not hatred of the people, but hatred of sin).

## So Why did Jesus tell parables?

Let's look at what Jesus Himself said about His parables:

> Matthew 13:10: *And the disciples came, and said unto him, Why speakest thou unto them in parables?*
> 11: *He answered and said unto them, Because it is given unto you to know the mysteries of the kingdom of heaven, but to them it is not given.*
> 12: *For whosoever hath, to him shall be given, and he shall have more abundance: but whosoever hath not, from him shall be taken away even that he hath.*
> 13: *Therefore speak I to them in parables: because*

*they seeing see not; and hearing they hear not, neither do they understand.* 14: *And in them is fulfilled the prophecy of Esaias, which saith, By hearing ye shall hear, and shall not understand; and seeing ye shall see, and shall not perceive:* 15: *For this people's heart is waxed gross, and their ears are dull of hearing, and their eyes they have closed; lest at any time they should see with their eyes, and hear with their ears, and should understand with their heart, and should be converted, and I should heal them.* 16: *But blessed are your eyes, for they see: and your ears, for they hear.*

Matthew 13:34: *All these things spake Jesus unto the multitude in parables; and without a parable spake he not unto them:* 35: *That it might be fulfilled which was spoken by the prophet, saying, I will open my mouth in parables; I will utter things which have been kept secret from the foundation of the world.* 36: *Then Jesus sent the multitude away, and went into the house: and his disciples came unto him, saying, Declare unto us the parable of the tares of the field.*

In other words: Jesus told parables to the hardhearted, spiritually dull, and rebellious who had already rejected His previous message of repentance.

If you only tell parables, you might as well just say "Stay Blind and Dumb and Deaf"

After Jesus told parables to the masses, He then INTERPRETED parables to His DISCIPLES. Then when He died on the cross and rose from the dead, He told His disciples to go MAKE MORE DISCIPLES.

He did not tell them to go minister parables and make lots of money, but to go make more disciples. Those disciples would then pass on the CLEAR INTERPRETATION to make more disciples.

So the key to ministry with parables is not the parable, but it is the CLEAR INTERPRETATION. If you are telling parables without giving the CLEAR and Direct INTERPRETATION of the parable, you are not following Jesus Christ Ministry Techniques for making disciples.

I encourage you – don't just speak the language of the world – bring them into the concepts of the Kingdom of God.

## TO SUM IT UP

There's nothing wrong with building relationships and having compassion. There's also nothing wrong with harsh warnings and repentance preaching. Mature, Spirit-led Christians use **BOTH**, not just one or the other. When it comes to ministry, the greatest example is Jesus Christ the King.

### Interpretation

That dream was pretty self-explanatory because it was given to us specifically when we were volunteering with The Call and Lou Engle, who is a modern-day John the Baptist, trying to turn America back to God. He and his staff are doing a great job at that work. They also are excellent at interpreting the dreams that are given to them and follow the Lord's Word.

But in a general sense it symbolizes a generation waiting to be entertained when God is calling for repentance. It symbolizes a generation being raised by demons, and being oppressed by abominations, while the elders are unaware. We must take authority and cry out to the Lord, and cry out against sin. We must **Repent** and turn the opposite direction with urgency.

# Application

**We Repent for Toleration of Jezebel's Doctrine** - toleration of sin, seduction, fornication, and compromise in life, dress, music:

- Tolerating pornography, lustful looks, and lustful entertainment.
- Tolerating sexual and seductive dress.
- Tolerating covetousness and a money focus over God
- Tolerating so-called Christian movies that are filled with adultery and sin, and foolish talk, with no anointing for deliverance.
- Tolerating Music and Ministry that mixes, and partners with the World (fornication).
- Tolerating Music and Ministry that copies and follows the World (teaching God's servants to eat food that has been sacrificed to idols).
- Tolerating Christian music that is a direct copycat of secular idolatry, uncreative, unoriginal. Regurgitating food offered to idols, and feeding it to God's people.
- Tolerating political lies and partnering with political liars to gain influence.

**We repent and we are turning our hearts back to our Holy, Pure, and Patient God who is a Consuming Fire!**

### Benefits of turning back to God:

-More effectiveness in our ministry gifts
-More power in our music
-More effectiveness in our discipleship
-More power over the nations
-More influence in the world for the Kingdom

*Revelations 2:23 And I will kill her [Jezebel's] children with death; and all the churches shall know that I am he which searcheth the reins and hearts: and I will give unto every one of you according to your works. 24 But unto you I say , and unto the rest in Thyatira, as many as have not this doctrine, and which have not known the depths of Satan, as they speak ; I will* *put upon you none other burden. 25 But that which ye have already hold fast till I come . 26 <u>And he that overcometh, and keepeth my works unto the end, to him will I give power over the nations</u>: 27 And he shall rule them with a rod of iron; as the vessels of a potter shall they be broken to shivers : even as I received of my Father. 28 And <u>I will give him the morning star</u>.*

---

**We Repent for Judas's Pragmatism and Betrayal with a Kiss** - Betraying the Purpose of Gods Ministries thru pragmatism, putting our thoughts over God's purpose. God still gets His purpose done anyway, but woe to the person used by Satan to betray the will of God. God has enough mercy to cover us, but only if we turn our hearts completely back to Him:

- We Betray God's purpose for finances when we purposefully limit God's increase in our life purposes. Earthly mindedness makes us think backwards. Purpose creates income, income doesn't create purpose.
- We Betray God's purpose for the ministry of our single lives when we live for ourselves. When we date around and do frivolous things that don't produce disciples for Christ, or Godly marriages for the Kingdom of God (1 Corinthians 7).
- We Betray Gods purpose for the ministry of our marriages with adultery and divorce.
- We Betray God's purpose for family when we allow and loose the **mentality** that is the seedbed of abortion – birth control and family planning.
  - Abortion came from Birth Control and Family Planning.
  - Birth Control and Family Planning came from Eugenics, which was man attempting to control who lives based on his own thoughts of financial usefulness and racial prejudices.
  - Eugenics came from Racism, Darwinisim, Humanism, and Atheism. At its core, it's

idolatry of the mind over God. Man rejected God, therefore sought to take control over the population of humans who are made in the image of God, based on their own thoughts.

- We blame abortion on the government, but we have the laws of abortion in our hearts.
- God is more jealous for changing the laws of our hearts than changing the laws of the land.

- We Betray God's purpose for our families when we decide not to allow God to produce the Godly seed that He desires. We believe the lie that children are a loss, when God says they are a blessing, a profit (Malach 2, Ps 127).
- We Betray God's purpose for our ministries when we change our message to fit the people, instead of changing the people to fit the message, the Word of God (Luke 3).
- We Betray God's purpose of our household ministry of hospitality by living isolated lives of entertainment instead of fellowshipping daily house to house.
- We Betray the purpose of the Father's House when we allow it to be a place where thieves can hide, instead of a House of Prayer for every ethnic group (John 2).

## We repent and we are turning our hearts back to the Only Wise and Merciful God!

### Benefits of Turning our hearts back to God:

-We will see that God's wisdom was greater than ours, with better results.

-We will experience His provision and blessing way more than we could have expected.

-The wealth of the wicked will finally come to us when we obey His purposes instead of ours.

-We will have children that will win their generation.

*Psalms 127:1 Except the LORD build the house, they labour in vain that build it: except the LORD keep the city, the watchman waketh but in vain. 2 It is vain for you to rise up early , to sit up late , to eat the bread of sorrows: for so he giveth his beloved sleep. 3 Lo,* *children are an heritage of the LORD: and the fruit of the womb is his reward. 4 As <u>arrows are in the hand of a mighty man; so are children of the youth</u>. 5 Happy is the man that hath his quiver full of them: they shall not be ashamed, but they shall speak with the enemies in the gate.*

**We Repent from Dog-tongues and Wolf-packs**: gossip, slander, using our tongues against our brothers. Ministries whose purpose is to tear down and steal from other ministries:

- We have authority over the atmosphere in our cities. Why are they so violent? How is gang warfare any different from using our tongues against others?
- We have sat in our churches and spoken against other races. We sit in fellowships and speak negatively about our brothers, spreading gossip and slander like dogs.
- Our tongues are our weapon, we kill people all the time. But when violence increases in the city, we wonder why?
- In many churches, every sermon has a "diss" of someone else's ministry in it. "That big church" "That small church" "That Baptist dollar" "Those Holy rollers". "White people."
- We sit in packs like wolves and kill others with our tongues, but then shake our head when the streets reflect the same violence.

**We repent and we are turning our hearts back to our Perfect Father in Heaven!**

**Benefits of Turning our hearts back to God:**

-More authority in our words.
-More fellowship with God.
-More peace in the Body of Christ, and in the community.
-More growth and spiritual edification.

*Psalms 50:19 Thou givest thy mouth to evil, and thy tongue frameth deceit. 20 Thou sittest and speakest against thy brother; thou slanderest thine own mother's son. 21 These things hast thou done , and I kept silence ; thou thoughtest that I was altogether such an one as thyself: but I will reprove thee, and set them in order before thine eyes. 22 Now consider this, ye that forget God, lest I tear you in pieces , and there be none to deliver . 23* <u>*Whoso offereth praise glorifieth me: and to him that ordereth his conversation aright will I shew the salvation of God.*</u>

**We Repent from being Dead Men's Bones & Hypocrites**:, worshipping traditions and Dead Men instead of following the Holy Ghost. Hypocrisy and being actors in real life:

- Putting our organizational and non-biblical traditions over Gods commandment for Unity of the Spirit in Jesus Christ and in Truth.
- Worshipping dead men's bones instead of relating all doctrine to the present testimony of Jesus Christ for today.
- We need to honor the old, and support the new. Both the New Wine and the Old wine can be preserved. Return the hearts of the Fathers to the Children, and the Hearts of the Children to the Fathers.
- Resisting the Holy Ghost instead of at least supporting the new things that God Sovereignly does in each generation. Traditions make the Word of God void of power.
- Being actors in real life, performing ministry but not living it in our hearts.

**We repent and we are turning our hearts back to the Living God!**

### Benefits of turning our hearts back to God:

-A living relationship with God, no need for masks.
-Less shame for the Body of Christ from fake actors.
-Holy Spirit effectiveness and power on our message.
-Children that are saved.
-Children that fulfill their calling in their generation.

*Isaiah 59:21 As for me, this is my covenant with them, saith the LORD; <u>My spirit</u> that is upon thee, and <u>my words</u> which I have put in thy mouth, shall not depart out of thy mouth, nor out of the mouth of thy seed, nor out of the mouth of thy seed's seed, saith the LORD, from henceforth and for ever.*

**We Repent for following Babylon Business Principles in the Kingdom of God**: brand warfare, usury, false balances, manipulation, slavery, witchcraft (pharmakia):

- Building our brands over being concerned with people.
- Putting profit before truth.
- Not keeping communication and transactions in simplicity.
- Defrauding each other to the point where we need lawyers to judge.
- Embracing usury and debt, enslaving Gods' people.
- Embracing systems of slavery, chattel, political, geological, financial, or spiritual.

**We repent and we are turning our hearts back to the Lord of the Harvest!**

**Benefits of turning our hearts back to God:**

-Wealth of the wicked laid up for us when we are just.
-Savings leading to financial freedom for the Body of Christ.
-Giving to the poor and true social justice will bless people all over the world.
-We will have businesses that employ and disciple the nations of the earth.
-We will own property and responsible businesses that take care of God's earth as stewards.

*Revelations 18:3 For all nations have drunk of the wine of the wrath of her fornication, and the kings of the earth have committed fornication with her, and the merchants of the earth are waxed rich through the abundance of her delicacies. 4 And I heard another voice from heaven, saying, Come out of her, my people, that ye be not partakers of her sins, and that ye receive not of her plagues. 5 For her sins have reached unto heaven, and God hath remembered her iniquities.*

**We Repent for Division and Allowing Thieves in the House of Prayer**: racial division and denominational division, not being a house of prayer for all nations:

- Being the world's best example of racial division on every Sunday.
- Being a place where thieves can hide, instead of a house of prayer for every ethnic group. Our "di-vision" makes our vision smaller, and therefore we don't feel the need to pray night and day for all nations.
- This is also related to Judas and Jezebel, because it has to do with the purpose of God for the Church, and also the Music Ministry. If thieves steal the house of prayer from the Church, it's a den of thieves. If Levites can't or won't be employed to worship God day & night, Jezebel and Judas have victory over them and steals their calling.
- The House of Prayer for every nation requires unity, regionally and racially.
- Dividing ourselves from each other instead of finding agreement in our different roles.

**We repent and we are turning our hearts back to our God who sits on the Throne and the Lamb who is Worthy of all Power, Riches, Wisdom, Strength, Honor, Glory, and Blessing.**

**Benefits of turning our hearts back to God:**

-We reflect heaven, therefore attract the world to God.
-The harvest comes in through unity and prayer.
-The world will believe when we become one.

*John 17:16 They are not of the world, even as I am not of the world. 17 Sanctify them through thy truth: thy word is truth. 18 As thou hast sent me into the world, even so have I also sent them into the world.*

*19 And for their sakes I sanctify myself, that they also might be sanctified through the truth. 20 Neither pray I for these alone, but for them also which shall believe on me through their word; 21 That they all may be one; as thou, Father, art in me, and I in thee, that they also may be one in us: <u>that the world may believe that thou hast sent me.</u>*

**Let's turn our hearts back to Our God! Let's Chop Off the Heads of the Giants, Snakes, and Dogs of the Enemy and Hold fast to the One Head, which is Jesus Christ!**

# 10

# LIFTING UP JESUS CHRIST THE HEAD OF THE CHURCH

### Who Is the Head?

> *Colossians 2:15 And having spoiled principalities and powers, he made a shew of them openly \*, triumphing over them in it. 16 Let no man therefore judge you in meat, or in drink, or in respect of an holyday, or of the new moon, or of the sabbath days: 17 Which are a shadow of things to come ; but the body is of Christ. 18 Let no man beguile you of your reward in a voluntary humility and <u>worshipping of angels [messengers],</u> intruding into those things which he hath not seen , vainly puffed up by his fleshly mind, 19 And <u>not holding the Head,</u> from which all the body by joints and bands having nourishment ministered , and knit together , increaseth with the increase of God.*

Jesus Christ is the King, He's the one that has beaten the principalities and powers, and He is in charge of His Church. Don't let anyone trick you out of your reward by getting you to follow their **religious traditions**, or their **anti-Christ ideas that don't come from the Bible**. Don't let anyone trick you out of your rewards in Christ by getting you to **worship messengers**, whether they be spirit angels, or human messengers. Hold fast to the Head, which is Jesus Christ!

## Jesus Christ, Man of Sorrows

*Isaiah 53:1 Who has believed our report? And to whom has the arm of the LORD been revealed? 2 For He shall grow up before Him as a tender plant, And as a root out of dry ground. He has no form or comeliness: And when we see Him, There is no beauty that we should desire Him. 3 He is despised and rejected by men, A Man of sorrows and acquainted with grief. And we hid, as it were, our faces from Him; He was despised, and we did not esteem Him.*

Jesus Christ did not always have a happy life. Jesus Christ did not have earthly glory or beauty to make people think He was the Messiah. Jesus Christ was a sorrowful man, full of grief, rejected and despised.

**Sorrow:** Physical and mental pain

## What was the Sorrow of Christ?

You are being beaten, slapped, spat on, hated and cursed by those you are giving your life for? What was the sorrow of Christ? You spend years pouring yourself into a group of people who vow to follow you and be with you, and in your hour of need they all abandon you? What was the sorrow of Christ? Hours before you are captured, you crying out to God in great distress and pain, and your followers are asleep? What was the sorrow of Christ? Jerusalem, the people God had pursued for thousands of years, who waited for the Messiah, does not even receive or recognize Him, though He left the right hand of the Father to show them the way? What was the sorrow of Christ? Our sorrows, that he carried.

**Grief:** Sickness, disease, sadness, grief

## What was the Grief of Christ?

That He bore in His body the sins of the world. He was perfect and NEVER committed sin, yet he was beaten so badly he was disfigured more than any man - for your sin and mine. The cross He suffered allows our healing today. Our grief He bore.

> *Isaiah 53:4 Surely he hath borne our griefs, and carried our sorrows: yet we did esteem him stricken, smitten of God, and afflicted. 5But he was wounded for our transgressions, he was bruised for our iniquities: the chastisement of our peace was upon him; and with his stripes we are healed.*

So we see that Jesus was full of sorrow, grief, rejection from those He came to save! Since Jesus had such a hard life, did He seek to make it better? Was He seeking and reading on how to have His best life now? No, even still, Jesus sought to do the will of the Father.

> *John 4:34 Jesus saith unto them, My meat is to do the will of him that sent me, and to finish his work.*

Jesus connection to the Father was so great, His love, devotion and faithfulness to Him were unmatched. He did all to please Him. This is our cue. We need not search out comfort, we need not search out vain and temporal happiness, but we have to seek the will of the Father, Jesus showed us the way.

After Christ's obedience was fulfilled did He not rise with all power? Did He not have total victory over death, hell and the grave? Jesus is definitely not suffering any longer. He is seated on the right hand of the Father forever. We should not expect half the grief and sorrow that Christ suffered, and God does promise to take care of us, and reward us in this life AND in the life to come for the things we give up or lose for His sake. He also promises us Joy in our fruitfulness and says we can be of good cheer, for He has overcome the world. But the principle is that we do not SEEK the pleasures of life, but the will of the Father, this is what Jesus did. He had the transgression of the entire world laid on Him, He did not seek to relieve Himself from it, but He sought how He might fulfill obedience to God's purpose for His life. He sought how to fulfill the scriptures that had prophesied of Him. And even when Peter said with good intentions that Jesus should not suffer, trying to show Him comfort and pity, Jesus rebuked Him, called Him Satan, and told Peter that he did not savor the things of God, but the things of man.

> *Matthew 16:21 From that time Jesus began to show to His disciples that He must go to Jerusalem, and suffer many things from the elders and chief priests and scribes, and be killed, and be raised the third day. 22 Then Peter took Him aside and began to rebuke Him, saying, "Far be it from You, Lord; this shall not happen to You!" 23 But He turned and said to Peter, "Get behind Me, Satan! You are an offense to Me, for you are not mindful of the things of God, but the things of men." 24 Then Jesus said to His disciples, "If anyone desires to come after Me, let him deny himself, and take up his cross, and follow Me. 25 For whoever desires to save his life will lose it, but whoever loses his life for My sake will find it. 26 For what profit is it to a man if he gains the whole world, and loses his own soul? Or what will a man give in exchange for his soul? 27 For the Son of Man will come in the glory of His Father with His angels, and then He will reward each according to his works.*

Though Jesus had many sorrows we cannot even imagine, His focus was pleasing God, and His victory came from it. Victory will spring from it eternally as He receives His bride and rules and reigns over heaven and earth. So we must follow suit and not look for the easy way, or the comfortable way, but we must savor the things that be of God, working to fulfill God's call, not our own desires.

> *Isaiah 53:10 Yet it pleased the LORD to bruise him; he hath put him to grief : when thou shalt make his soul an offering for sin, <u>he shall see his seed, he shall prolong his days, and the pleasure of the LORD shall prosper in his hand.</u> 11 He shall see of the travail of his soul, and <u>shall be satisfied</u> : by his knowledge shall my righteous servant justify many; for he shall bear their iniquities. 12 Therefore <u>will I divide him a portion with the great, and he shall divide the spoil with the strong;</u> because he hath poured out his soul unto death: and he was numbered with the transgressors ; and he bare the sin of many, and made intercession for the transgressors.*

In Isaiah 53 it continues and shows that Jesus will be completely satisfied from His suffering and His intercession, and He will be rewarded and considered great and strong in the very place where He suffered.

**Jesus Christ, Man of Sorrow. Jesus Christ, Resurrected and Victorious Forever!**

**Jesus, the Beautiful One**

We have to take our eyes off man...Jesus is the beautiful one! He alone deserves our gaze, our adoration and our praise! HE ALONE IS WORTHY! HE IS THE ONLY ONE WHO HAS SACRIFICED FOR ALL.

Our gaze of adoration toward man is part of what has led to the demise of many Christian artists, pastors, etc. As we admire them, they become filled with pride; they begin relying on self instead of God, get full of the flesh, and are overtaken.

Also, when we focus on man our hearts are not able to receive the full revelation of Jesus Christ that transforms our hearts and spirits. Because God will have NO other God's before Him, and when you set your hopes on man, you put that man before God and it is a form of adultery.

Another distraction from the beauty of Jesus is earthly anxiety. Jesus is the beautiful one, Jesus is the powerful one. Earthly anxiety robs our hearts from focusing on Christ and chokes the word of God from being planted in our hearts (**Matthew 6:25-34, Luke 8:14, Luke 21:34**).

As the people of God, the desire of HIS heart, return their gaze, their affections, their longings back to Jesus Christ, the beautiful One, things will truly change.

The children of Israel were afraid of going before the Lord, because He is Holy. They told Moses to go for them. So that means they did not have perfect love for God (**Exodus 20, 32**) Perfect love casts out fear, **1 John 4:17-19**! When Isaiah saw the Lord high and lifted up, He said woe is me, I am a man of unclean lips (**Isaiah 6**). When we are in God's presence we are naked before Him and our flesh becomes uncomfortable. So then we want others to go before GOD for us, we want to glean from their revelation instead of getting before God ourselves. God is the lover, but also the refiner, pruner, chastener.

So then, because we are not close to God ourselves, loving Him with all of our heart mind soul and strength... we still long for God. We are afraid to get too close, so we cling to what seems like God and elevate them to the place of God and worship the creature rather than the Creator. The Children of Israel did not want to draw close to God, they wanted Moses to go for them, so their hearts were idle, not focusing on the beauty of Jesus, because Moses was on the mountain, beholding God for them. So what happened? They created an idol made of Gold to worship instead. The idol has no holiness to fear so it is easier to be in its presence.

> *2 Corinthians 3:16 Nevertheless when it shall turn to the Lord, the vail shall be taken away . 17 Now the Lord is that Spirit: and where the Spirit of the Lord is, there is liberty. 18 But we all, with open face beholding as in a glass the glory of the Lord, are changed into the same image from glory to glory, even as by the Spirit of the Lord.*

I challenge myself, I challenge you, to retract our hearts from all things that steal our gaze, our focus from Jesus Christ the Beautiful One. Is it t.v? Is it facebook? Is it sports? What takes your focus, your heart gaze from the Holy God of Israel? When we focus on Christ we will be healed, cleansed, we will be blessed with greater revelation and understanding of who Christ is and how to love Him with all of our being.

> Luke 10:27 And he answering said, You shall love the Lord your God with all your heart, and with all your soul, and with all your strength, and with all your mind; and your neighbor as yourself.

Jesus is The Beautiful One. What owns your focus? Who holds your gaze? This is why He is so beautiful:

> Revelations 5 7And he came and took the book out of the right hand of him that sat upon the throne. 8And when he had taken the book, the four beasts and four and twenty elders fell down before the Lamb, having every one of them harps, and golden vials full of odours, which are the prayers of saints. 9And they sung a new song, saying, Thou art worthy to take the book, and to open the seals thereof: for thou wast slain, and hast redeemed us to God by thy blood out of every kindred, and tongue, and people, and nation; 10And hast made us unto our God kings and priests: and we shall reign on the earth. 11And I beheld, and I heard the voice of many angels round about the throne and the beasts and the elders: and the number of them was ten thousand times ten thousand, and thousands of thousands;
>
> 12Saying with a loud voice, Worthy is the Lamb that was slain to receive power, and riches, and wisdom, and strength, and honour, and glory, and blessing.

> <sup>13</sup>*And every creature which is in heaven, and on the earth, and under the earth, and such as are in the sea, and all that are in them, heard I saying, Blessing, and honour, and glory, and power, be unto him that sitteth upon the throne, and unto the Lamb for ever and ever.* <sup>14</sup>*And the four beasts said, Amen. And the four and twenty elders fell down and worshipped him that liveth for ever and ever.*

## Music and Ministry to Glorify the True Head, Which is Christ!

> *1 Corinthians 11:3 But I would have you know , that **the head of every man is Christ;** and the head of the woman is the man; and the head of Christ is God.*

## It all starts with understanding God.

God is **Creator**. God is **Truth**. God is **Love**.

Satan is NOT **Creator**. Satan is NOT equal and opposite to God, he is only a depraved (hopelessly wicked) **create**d being. Satan cannot **create** Good or Evil. But Satan is a **liar** (John 8). Satan also is a **deceive**r (2 John 1). He comes to steal, kill, and destroy (John 10).

God – **Creates**. Satan – **Steals**.

God – Is **Truth**. Satan – Is a **Lie**.

God – **Loves**. Satan – **Deceives**.

## What's Really Important in Music and Ministry?

The most important characteristics in a minister or musician are Truth, then Character, then Creative Power. Truth is more important than character. Character is more important than Creative Power.

Why, you say?

Well I'm glad you asked.

**Truth** is of highest importance. God Himself ranks His Word as even Higher than His name (Psalms 138). Character flaws can be forgiven and disciplined - but lies are from Satan, and can never be redeemed. David may have sinned with Bathsheba, but his inspired writings are still Scripture. God's truth can never be erased. Heaven and Earth may pass away, but God's Word will never pass away. Someone could seem like they have all the love, affection, and kindness in the world - but if they teach lies against God's truth, judgment day will find them out, and those who follow them will suffer greatly.

**Character** ranks next in importance, because character shows obedience to the Truth, and it shows the Love of God. Why would you want to be a representative of God's Truth and Love, and refuse to do it? Those are called hypocrites... Jesus Christ rebuked them. As a matter of fact, Jesus even said "Do What they say" (because they speak truth). "But do not do what they do." Because they are actors with little character or Love. I'm sure you know many ministers and musical artists that God has exposed for speaking some truth, but being a sinner behind closed doors.

**Creative Power** ranks next in order. Creative power represents the power of the Holy Spirit to be creative, do miracles, manifest gifts of the Spirit, etc. These are good things because they come from God, but they are not as important as Truth, or (Character) Love. This is because God is so generous; He can give creative power to any human that is made in the image of God. Satan can lie and deceive those people into using God's creative power for evil purposes.

This is why the bible says that Pharoah's magicians, Jannes and Jambres, did miracles to try and oppose the Truth. The truth is most important. The important part was not that they could do miracles - it was the purpose for which they did the miracles (2 Timothy 3:8).

There are people that use God's gifts, and God's power for evil purposes. In the same way, you have seen those with creative gifts and musical gifts from God, that are deceived into using it for Satan's purposes. Creative power is a good thing. When that good thing is stolen by the devil, it's used for evil.

## How does this relate to music and ministry?

Our job as believers in Christ is to destroy the works of the enemy (1 John 3:8).

We destroy the works of the enemy by replacing Lies with Truth, replacing Deception with Love, and tapping into a flow of God's Creative Power to bless those around us.

What does this look like? It looks like Jesus. It looks like writing lyrics and preaching messages that are filled with the Word of God. It looks like Jesus not tolerating or agreeing with deception. It looks like Jesus loving people that are deceived by snatching them out of deception through repentance, casting out demons, and then giving them something specific to replace their deception with. It looks like Jesus feeding the hungry and clothing the naked, and being moved with compassion. It looks like Jesus laboring in prayer and faith with the Holy Spirit for creative power, healing power, miracle power, and the baptisms of God to bless all that will receive. When we gaze upon Jesus we will have endless Truth, Love, and Creative Power to do the work we need to do.

**Christ is our Source! His Word is exalted even above His name and none of it will be hidden. He is building His people together as living stones into a House of Prayer for all nations. He is thrusting out laborers into His harvest!**

# 11

# THE PROTEST:
# IF YOU REALLY LOVE JESUS -
# THE SPIRIT OF ELIJAH COMES FIRST

**Shereena's Dream**

*The Protest :  Fall or Winter 2011*
*I dreamed that I was at a Christian Café. There was food, music and different people ministering their talents. The place felt a bit strange and I could see out the front window and there were people across the street protesting against the café. However, everyone inside seemed to be true Christians and they were having a good time so I ignored the uneasiness I felt and ignored the protesters. Everyone was sitting at quaint little café tables, enjoying their food and conversations, then five or six identical young African American girls went up to the front to do a praise dance. They were dressed in typical praise dance outfits (long flowing skirts, leotards, and dance shoes), their dance seemed normal and they were giving praises to God. But then, identical large women dressed in dark metallic dresses that were heavily adorned with make-up and jewelry walked to the front and lined up behind the girls who were praise dancing. There were as many large grown women as there were young praise dancers. When the women lined up behind the praise dancers, the praise dancers turned and bowed down to them. As soon as they did that I got up and walked out of the café and went across the street and joined the protesters.*

*We were standing on a green, grassy lawn, some of us were holding up signs and we were standing against the compromise of the "Christian" café. As I was standing in the protest, a black limousine came and picked me up. I got in the back seat of the limo. There was a chauffeur I could not see and a very large man riding in the front passenger seat next to the chauffeur. The man in the passenger seat was very large and very rich. He was dressed in a dark colored suit with a white shirt and a neck tie. He was very serious. I could see his form, but I never saw His face. When I got in the limo the chauffeur started to drive. The man in the passenger seat told me He would fund me as long as I was protesting against the café, and He pulled out His check book and began to write me a check (and I felt as if the check was the first of many that would follow). Then He told me that I could now be called Lily [In real life I had been praying to God for a new name for many years]. Then the driver circled the block and dropped me back off with the protesters.*

*Monster's Ball: June 2012*
*I dreamed that a big Christian hip-hop concert was coming to town and EVERYONE was going except me. I knew that the artists were not right, that they were turning people away from righteousness. So I was literally the only one in town not going to the concert. It was night time and I was sitting at a table with a Christian friend and a few others, when it was time for the concert to start everyone got up and went. I stood alone. Then I looked and I saw the concert artists sitting in a row on a bench. They were dressed in black, with darkness all around them. They had on masks with knives and sharp metal objects protruding from them, the masks were locked onto their faces with steel metal bands around their necks. The knives and sharp objects that protruded from the masks were covered in blood. The artists looked like creatures from a horror movie. And it also seemed as if their minds were gone, they were totally zoned out. My Christian friend then stood next to me, and many other concert goers. I pulled my friend over to me and showed her the artists. I asked her "what do they all have in common? They are all covered in blood". My friend and everyone else acted as if they could not*

*see the truth about the artists, like nothing was wrong. I stayed out of the concert; I think I prayed while the concert was going on.*

*Then the scene changed. It was daylight outside and the concert had passed. And one of the artists from the concert came out of a building and he was totally clean and new! He looked so refreshed and happy. He was wearing a blue polo shirt and white shorts. He came up to me and gave me a huge brotherly hug and thanked me for praying for him. He took me into the building he came out of and there was a banquet going on. He sat me next him at the table he was sitting at. He told everyone at the table that I had prayed for him, he was so grateful. There were sinners and saved people at the table. The artist had given me a place of honor sitting next to him, because instead of being entertained by him when he was perpetuating darkness as light, I exposed his lie and prayed for him, and he was delivered by God!!!*

*Ducking & Hiding: August 2012*
*I dreamed that we were having church in a room that was above the Fox Theatre or something like it. Since the theatre had so many secular concerts and events and brought so much sin into the city via performances, we were speaking and proclaiming over it. There was a Snoop Dogg concert that was going to start as we were speaking and proclaiming over the facility, and we could see through the wall to the side walk in front of the building. And as we were speaking and proclaiming Snoop Dogg was in front of the building having to duck under our words. Our proclamations were affecting him and the concert he was putting on, although they pretended like we did not even exist. He was holding his infant son in his arms as he was going under our words. And there was also a young black man who was with Snoop; Snoop was teaching the young man how to go under our words also.*

## Scripture

### A Confrontational Preaching Anointing

If you love Jesus and want him back soon, think about this: Malachi 4. The Spirit of Elijah comes first.

> *Malachi 4 ⁴Remember ye the law of Moses my servant, which I commanded unto him in Horeb for all Israel, with the statutes and judgments. ⁵Behold, I* **will send you Elijah the prophet** <u>*before the coming of the great and dreadful day of the LORD*</u>: *⁶And he shall turn the heart of the fathers to the children, and the heart of the children to their fathers, lest I come and smite the earth with a curse.*

Jesus also confirmed this: "Elijah comes first, and restores all things" (Matthew 17:11).

The Spirit of Elijah did not turn hearts of people by preaching a message on 'turning your hearts'. He didn't say "Fathers, turn you hearts back to your children. Children, now you go and turn your hearts back to your fathers." Even though those would have been very good messages, that's not what it took.

When he prayed, he told God "Let them know that you have turned their hearts again." But that's not what he said to the people. He didn't say "Everybody turn your hearts back to God please."

What did Elijah actually do?

> *1 Kings 18:17 And it came to pass, when Ahab saw Elijah, that Ahab said unto him, Art thou he that troubleth Israel? 18 And he answered, I have not troubled Israel; but thou, and*

*thy father's house, in that ye have forsaken the commandments of the LORD, and thou hast followed Baalim.19 Now therefore send , and gather to me all Israel unto mount Carmel, and the prophets of Baal four hundred and fifty, and the prophets of*

*the groves four hundred, which eat at Jezebel's table. 20 So Ahab sent unto all the children of Israel, and gathered the prophets toge ther unto mount Carmel. 21 And Elijah came unto all the people, and said , How long halt ye between two opinions? if the LORD be God, follow him: but if Baal, then follow him. And the people answered him not a word.22 Then said Elijah unto the people, I, even I only, remain a prophet of*

*the LORD; but Baal'sprophets are four hundred and fi fty men. 23 Let them therefore give us two bullocks; and let them choose one bullock for themselves, and cut it in pieces , and lay it on wood, and put no fire under: and I will dress the other bullock, and lay it on wood, and put no fire under: 24 And call ye on the name of your gods, and I will call on the name of the LORD: and the God that answereth by fire, let him be God. And all the people answered and said , It is well spoken. 25 And Elijah said unto the prophets of Baal, Choose you one bullock for yourselves, and dress it first; for ye are many; and call on the name of your gods, but put no fire under. 26 And they took the bullock which was given them, and they dressed it, and called on the name of Baal from morning even until noon, saying ,*

*O Baal, hear us. But there was no voice, nor any that answered . And they leaped upon the altar which was made . 27 And it came to pass at noon, that Elijah mocked them,*

*and said , Cry aloud : for he is a god; either he is talking, or he is pursuing, or he is in a journey, or peradventure he sleepeth, and must be awaked. 28 And they cried aloud , and cut themselves after their manner with knives and lancets, till the blood gushed out upon them. 29 And it came to pass, when midday was past , and they prophesied until the time of the offeringof the evening sacrifice, that there was neither voice, nor any to answer , nor any that regarded.30And Elijah said unto all the people, Come near unto me. And all the people came near unto him. And he repaired the altar of the LORD that was broken down .31And Elijah took twelve stones, accor ding to the number of the tribes of the sons of Jacob, unto whom the word of the LORD came, saying , Israel shall be thy name:32And with the stones he built an altar in the name of the LORD: and he made a trench about the altar, as great as would contain two measures of seed.33And he put the wood in order , and cut the bullock in pieces, and laid him on the wood, and said, Fill four barrels with water, and p our it on the burnt sacrifice, and on the wood.34And he said , Do it the second time . And they did it the second time . And he said , Do it the third time . And they did it the third time .35 And the water ran round about the altar; and he filled the trench also with water. 36 And it came to pass at the time of the offering of the evening sacrifice, that Elijah the prophet came near, and said, LORD God of Abraham, Isaac, and of Israel, let it be known this day that thou art God in Israel, and that I am thy servant, and that I have done all these things at thy word. 37 Hear me, O LORD, hear me, that this people may know that thou art the LORD God, and that thou hast turned their heart back again. 38 Then the fire of the LORD fell, and consumed the burnt sacrifice, and the wood, and the stones, and the dust, and licked up the water that was in the trench. 39 And when all the people saw it, they fell on their faces: and they said, The LORD, he is the God; the LORD, he is the God. 40 And Elijah said to them, Take the prophets of Baal; let not one of them escape. And they took them: and Elijah brought them down to the brook Kishon, and slew them there. 41And Elijah said unto Ahab, Get up, eat and drink; for there is a sound of abundance of rain.*

The Spirit of Elijah set up a confrontation with idols and false prophets in the Kingdom. He let them have the stage for as much time as they wanted. He let them set up their altars. He let them have the advantage, 450 to 1. He clowned them. He gave himself a disadvantage, making his altar especially hard to "catch fire" by dousing it with water.

What did the crowd say when it was time for the confrontation – "not a word." They really didn't know whether to worship God or Baal (the idol of money & power) (1 Kings 18:21).

But when the fire came, the people automatically said "the Lord is God." Then Elijah killed all the false prophets.

## Sometimes the Trouble Maker is Really the Peacemaker

Ahab called Elijah the "troubler of Israel" because he wanted to continue mixing their idolatry, Baal worship and murderous ways into the kingdom of God without interruption.

But really Ahab and Elijah were the troublers of Israel, and Elijah was sent by God to bring true peace back to the kingdom of God. Jesus didn't say to be a peacekeeper... Sometimes you have to confront things and be a peaceMAKER.

> ***Matthew 5:9 Blessed are the peacemakers: for they shall be called the children of God.***

This is the same spirit of Elijah that manifested in John the Baptist before the first coming of Jesus the Messiah. He confronted the religious leaders of his day that really worshipped Baal (the god of money & power). They were good at getting money, but not good at loving God with real fruit. He gave himself a disadvantage – preaching in the desert instead of on a mountain or in the middle of the city, or the temple. His father was High Priest, he could have had an easy platform if he wanted. People came out to hear anyway and repent and be baptized, and he rebuked the false religious and political leaders of his day.

A **Confrontational Preaching Anointing** is what God will manifest before Christ's 2nd Coming also.

If you really love Jesus Christ and want to see Him soon, don't be scared to confront the false idols and false prophets of today. That's what is necessary to see revival, a great awakening, the last days harvest, and the 2nd coming of Jesus Christ. **Do you really love Jesus or not?**

Holiness Hastens the coming of the Lord (2 Peter 3:12). Does this mean that we can only support ministries that have never done anything wrong, ever? Of course not. But it does mean that when God administers correction through His Word, we have to obey God instead of men, and follow those who do the same.

### It's An Honor to Remain on the Narrow Road

It's an honor to remain on the narrow road that leads to life instead of the broad road that leads to destruction.

> *Matthew 7:13-14 Enter ye in at the strait gate: for wide is the gate, and **broad is the way, that leadeth to destruction, and many there be which go in thereat**: Because strait is the gate, and narrow is the way, which leadeth unto life, and few there be that find it.*

### False Prophets that Lead you on the Wide Road Are Sheep on the Outside, but They are Wolves Inside.

> *Matthew 7: 15 Beware of false prophets, which come to you in sheep's clothing, but <u>inwardly they are ravening wolves</u>. Ye shall know them by their fruits. Do men gather grapes of thorns, or figs of thistles? Even so every good tree bringeth forth good fruit; but a corrupt tree bringeth forth evil fruit. A good tree cannot bring forth evil fruit, neither can a corrupt tree bring forth good fruit. Every tree that bringeth not forth good fruit is hewn down, and cast into the fire. Wherefore by their fruits ye shall know them.*

**Many People on the Wide Road, Even Ones That Preach, Prophesy, Do Good Works and Call Jesus "Lord, Lord" Will Burn in Hell Because they Worked Iniquity.**

> *Matthew 7:21 Not every one that saith unto me, Lord, Lord, shall enter into the kingdom of heaven; but he that doeth the will of my Father which is in heaven. Many will say to me in that day, Lord, Lord, have we not prophesied in thy name? and in thy name have cast out devils? and in thy name done many wonderful works? And then will I profess unto them, I never knew you: depart from me, **ye that work iniquity.***

### What's the Difference between Sin and Iniquity?

Sin is the sickness. Iniquity is the virus. Sins are the symptoms, iniquity is what leads to the symptoms.

Sin is obvious, iniquity is hidden. Iniquity is what was found in Satan. "Iniquity was found in thee." (Ezekial 28:15) Satan is the original spreader of iniquity. He doesn't deal in the symptoms, he deals in the virus, the unobvious portion.

False prophets don't necessarily spread sin, that would be too obvious. But they do spread iniquity - they "work" iniquity. It's the iniquity that causes the sin to show up eventually, in many people. Some people hide the symptoms better than others.

That's why many people will call Jesus Lord Lord and do many many works in his name, but Jesus will say " depart from me I never knew you, you that "work" iniquity. "

They are hungry wolves that "work" iniquity and they do not do the will of our Father in heaven. And the "many" people that follow them on the broad road will be headed to destruction.

### Some Sheep on the Outside are Wolves on the Inside

What comes to your mind when you think of a wolf in sheep's clothing? Is it a wolf's snout with and fangs, with a white fluffy lambs wool coat that's a little too small, and lambs wool hat for the back of its head? Get that picture out of your head.

A wolf in sheep's clothing is not obvious. A wolf in sheep's clothing looks completely like a sheep on the outside, but **inside** they are hungry wolves.

### 2 Ways to Tell there's a Wolf in sheep's clothing:

1. Sheep start dying. God's people start to cool off, fall in sin, and be consumed spiritually. They still talk about Christ, but they compromise and are dead inside. The Beauty of Holiness is no longer important. You will know them by their fruit.
2. They start letting in other wolves into the flock  - wolves **without** sheep's clothing! They open the gate on the sly, at night, they use their influence in the church and start partnering and working with unbelievers.

This is why we have to protest!

### Narrower and Narrower

Did you ever notice how Jesus's road got narrower and narrower? Why do His followers want a road that gets wider and wider?

"Things are tight now, but if I stay faithful this road is going to get broader and wider in the future!" – Wrong.

"I can't wait for the day when I can get off this Narrow road! I'm believing for the day when I get blessed to Go Broad!" – Wrong.

As you walk with Christ, the path gets brighter and brighter because you have more revelation and light from the Holy Spirit on who Jesus Christ really is (Proverbs 4:18). You will see the path getting clearer and narrower, not broader and wider. If you switch to a broader road you are headed for destruction.

This is why we have to protest!

**It's So sad to see a Holy Movement turn into a Corrupted Market: We Are Not Like MANY Who Corrupt the Word of God**

Body of Christ please get the thieves out of the house of prayer and get the wolves out the sheepfold!!! Lives are at stake for our laziness!

God needs people who will die for the truth, not people who will corrupt and peddle the message.

> *2 Corinthians 2:17 For we are not as **many**, which **corrupt the word of God**: but as of sincerity, but as of God, in the sight of God speak we in Christ.*

In order to understand that scripture you have to understand the word "corrupt". It carries the connotation of watering down, to make extra profits.

> *Corrupt - Definition:*
>
> *1. to be a retailer, to peddle 2. to make money by selling anything a. to get sordid gain by dealing in anything, to do a thing for base gain b. to trade in the word of God 1. to try to get base gain by teaching divine truth c. to corrupt, to adulterate 1. peddlers were in the habit of adulterating their commodities for the sake of gain*
>
> *Origin: from kapelos (a huckster)*

Does that means Christians can't sell anything with biblical instruction in it?? Proverbs 11 says a blessing is on the head of him that sells his surplus food. Psalms 66 says "the Lord gave the word, great was the company of them that published it." Selling is not a necessarily a sin, in the correct context. But corrupting the Word of God is iniquity.

God has a message to get to a generation. His mercy endures forever, his truth to every generation. This message is hard, it's a cross, it may bring suffering or loss, it requires holiness and sacrifice.

You can be faithful to it, or you can corrupt it and peddle it.

"We'll reach more people without all that preaching and complicated truth."

"It's all about getting more people anyway, people don't want those spiritual extremes."

"Let's remix it with this secular idolatry so we get more attention."

"It's so hard to be a divider, let's just find the least common denominator, and brand it to as many people as possible."

"Doing it this way reaches more people, which means more money, and it's all about reaching people anyway."

All these types of thoughts are substituted for obedience. They seem wise, but they actually delay Gods true purposes and cause people to be led astray and burn in hell.

If you lead 100 people down a narrow road, and then swerve to the left, because the wide road – that looks like it's going the same way – fits 1000 people, then you have just led 1000 people off the narrow road that leads to life and onto the broad road that leads to destruction. Think about that.

Paul said that there were many false apostles that followed him around, corrupting his message and disguising themselves as wiser apostles. They were really messengers of Satan (2 Corinthians 11:13).

2 Corinthians, and even most of the new testament- is all about teaching true messengers to defend against false messengers that sneak in to corrupt the truth.

It's the same today, there are "many" who "peddle" and "corrupt" the word of God.

There are false messengers and blind leaders that don't see the beauty of holiness or see make a commitment to communicate the whole message; but they look at God's people and see a market to conquer and make more profitable by spiritual cost cutting and "cross cutting."

Their negative spiritual impact is mind-bogglingly huge, but they will never know, because they are spiritually blind. So they just "wait till judgement day" to find out that they were the workers of iniquity that Jesus never really knew (Matt 7), or that their work was as useless as hay & stubble (2 Cor 3).That's why true Servants of God must warn and be warned with aggressive vigilance.

In the book of Nehemiah, Tobias was the person who opposed and plotted against Nehemiah when he was building the walls of Jerusalem (symbolizing holiness and protection). But then after he failed to stop them, he did so much business with the Jews that they gave him a room in the temple, and kicked out the Levites - who God set up to be the power source of worship & prayer for the Kingdom of God - but they kicked them out for business reasons, of course. So the Levites were working in the fields and the thief and enemy of the truth was living in the temple.

Get the corrupters out of the temple! A generation could be lost if we don't get this right. True revival diverted and delayed means lost souls.

Corrupting the Word of God makes it easier to sell, but in the long run more people end up in hell. His ways are higher than our ways, and His thoughts are higher than our thoughts.

## When Deception Came to the Body of Christ

> **Proverbs 24:10** *If thou faint in the day of adversity, thy strength is small.*

When deception came to the Body of Christ, God was writing a book.

He was writing a book of those who supported and went along with it, and who stood against it.

He's writing a book of who said "Lord, Lord" and kept all the religious language but refused to obey Him... and He wrote down who obeyed Him and suffered the rejection of the world.

There is still time to repent with fruit, and get your name in the right column in God's book.

### You Have to Disciple the Few, Not Reach the Masses

The job of the false prophet is to reach the Masses with a corrupted message that is halfway true, and get praise and honor from men in his own generation. The pay is high, in the kingdom of man.

The job of the true messenger is to disciple the Few with a pure message that is lived in truth, and modeled to instruct God's remnant and change future generations. The pay is high, in the kingdom of God.

Are you saying that true messengers can't have success? No.

True Messengers wear success loosely, knowing that it's temporary and fleeting, and that praise from men will soon be reversed into hatred. They don't mind having success in discipling and teaching the remnant, but they know that success with the masses is a lie. If they get mass success – they don't hold on to it – they keep chasing higher levels of truth, purity, and creativity in God. The only thing they do with success is teach others how they got it.

False prophets get success and then try to keep it. They keep trying to stay on top and stay in control, worshipping their gift, talent, or formula, and end up totally deceived and prophesying for more success instead of for God.

> *Luke 16:15 And he said unto them, Ye are they which justify yourselves before men; but God knows y our hearts: for **that which is highly esteemed among men is abomination in the sight of God.***

> *John 7:7*
> *The world cannot hate you; but me it hateth , becaus e **I testify of it, that the works thereof are evil**.*

> *Galatians 1:10*
> *For do I now persuade men, or God? or do I seek to please men? for **if I yet pleased men, I should not be the servant of Christ**.*

> *Luke 6:22 Blessed are you when men hate you, and ostracize you, and insult you, and scorn your name as evil, for the sake of the Son of Man. 23 Be glad in that day and leap for joy, for behold, your reward is great in heaven. For **in the same way their fathers used to treat the prophets...***
> *26 **Woe to you when all men speak well of you, for their fathers used to treat the false prophets in the same way***

## The Protest is for the Few that are on the Path to Life, Not the Many that are on the Broad Road to Destruction

### Satan's Investment in Angels of Light

Satans biggest investment is not in obvious wickedness... The whole world already lies in his power (1 John 5:19). They sin because they love sin. His biggest investment is in corrupting, weakening, and compromising the righteous. Because they are the only ones with power to stop him. Think about it... Satan is not God's evil archenemy like some kind of comic book story. Satan is just a corrupted angel. God is unstoppable and God's people are unstoppable.

If I was Satan, my biggest investment would be to **make my unstoppable enemy weaker by corrupting him**. Give him success and acceptance in this world for watering down or corrupting his power and message. That way he can't really defeat me because he'll be powerless and he won't want to.

It would be best for him to be known as a minister of light so that i could spread a virus of iniquity and darkness into a generation of the righteous through him without people knowing it. That's why satan always sends wolves in sheep's clothing, and his ministers always appear righteous on the outside.

And anyone that refuses to be corrupted, those are the ones Satan threatens, tries to eliminate and kill. They get rejected by the system that Satan controls (the world).

Anyone that thinks Satan's biggest strategy is in things that are obviously evil doesn't understand the first thing about the nature if Satan. Satan is not obvious darkness, he's corrupted light. He's not obvious lies, he's watered down wisdom.

> *2 Corinthians 11:13-15  For such are false apostles, deceitful workers, transforming themselves into the apostles of Christ. And no marvel; for <u>Satan himself is transformed into an angel of light</u>. Therefore it is no great thing if his <u>ministers also be transformed as the ministers of righteousness</u>; whose end shall be according to their works.*

*Ezekiel 28:14-17 Thou art the anointed cherub that covereth; and I have set thee so: thou wast upon the holy mountain of God; thou hast walked up and down in the midst of the stones of fire. Thou wast perfect in thy ways from the day that thou wast created, till <u>iniquity was found in thee</u>. By the <u>multitude of thy merchandise</u> they <u>have filled the midst of thee with violence</u>, and thou hast sinned: therefore I will cast thee as profane out of the mountain of God: and I will destroy thee, O covering cherub, from the midst of the stones of fire. Thine heart was lifted up because of thy beauty, thou hast **corrupted thy wisdom by reason of thy brightness**: I will cast thee to the ground, I will lay thee before kings, that they may behold thee.*

---

Join the Protest. **God will Provide** for those that Protest Against <u>Satan's Investment</u> in Angels of Light.

## It's a Privilege Not to Be a Bastard

Correction by God is a privilege, it's not something to be ashamed of at all. Inversely, when you don't repent for correction, that's **not** something to be unashamed of.

Why? Because bastards don't get correction or repent, they just get their heart hardened in their error, and they succeed in sin, which is really failure.

*Exodus 7:13 And **he hardened Pharaoh's heart**, that he hearkened not unto them; as the LORD had said.*

*John 12:40 He hath blinded their eyes, and hardened their heart; that they should not see with their eyes, nor understand with their heart, and be converted, and I should heal them.*

*Hebrews 12 6 For whom the Lord loveth he chasteneth, and scourgeth every son whom he receiveth. 7 If ye endure chastening, God dealeth with you as with sons; for what son is he whom the father chasteneth not? 8 **But if ye be without chastisement, whereof all are partakers, then are ye bastards, and not sons**. 9 Furthermore we have had fathers of our flesh which corrected us, and we gave them reverence: shall we not much rather be in subjection unto the Father of spirits, and live?*

Once faced with the truth, those that don't repent are just proving themselves to be bastards instead of sons of God that get corrected. Don't be intimidated by those that have success in sin. Don't fall a victim to copouts that "nobody can really live it."

Our Father in Heaven desires obedience, holiness, and the Holy Spirit desires Christ formed in us. No cop outs and excuses, for His commandments are not grievous, and every idle word and deed will be accounted for on judgment day.

Jesus is waiting for the generation that seeks His face - not the generation of more excuses and copouts! So the King of Glory can come in (Psalms 24).

Everything is waiting, crying out and groaning, for the appearance of the true sons of God...So let the wolves dance with wolves and let the sheep follow the Shepherd! Manifest who you are in Christ!

The very earth is waiting for the true Sons of God – that are led by the Spirit of God, and kill the deeds of the flesh by the Holy Spirit – to appear (Romans 8).

When God gives correction, it's a privilege. If you repent, it means you are not a bastard, you are a son of God. If you have success in sin without real repentance, you are a spiritual bastard.

## Protesting Babies in Charge and Protesting Wolves

Bastards? Wolves? False Prophets? Man, this chapter sounds really harsh. What if they just don't know? What happened to the gentleness from Galatians 6?

Yes, we all had a time when we don't know. Please don't take all these harsh words as anger or malice. This isn't personal, this is spiritual. There is a generation at stake, and eternal lives are in the balance. The protest has to be clear and sober, because the consequences are serious. Spiritual surgery on the Body of Christ is tough, but it has to be done.

Some people say that when you bring correction, you don't have love. In God's eyes, the greater the love, the greater and more consistent the correction.

Also, these are all scriptural concepts, and they need to be FULLY TAUGHT and DECLARED with boldness. Teaching these scriptures is a way to restore and build up brethren with gentleness. Preaching them is a way to rescue people that have been a victim of the enemies deception. It allows people to correct themselves and repent according to the Word of God.

If you don't care when the wolf eats the sheep, why do you get mad when the shepherd kills the wolf? These are the spiritual checks and balances that keep the Body of Christ pure and growing. This is needed for spiritual correction and repentance.

When the sheep are being spiritually killed and consumed, nobody cares. Then when the Chief Shepherd does His job - everybody wants to act like it's time to be nice. That's because most people don't see with spiritual eyes, they only see an earthly minded perspective. So hirelings flee when they see the wolf. But the Chief Shepherd lays down His life for the sheep.

The Chief Shepherd also teaches the baby sheep. One of the marks of baby Christians is that they cannot discern between good & evil. But when truth is taught and communicated with Scriptural backup and Holy Spirit Revelation, babies have a responsibility for obedience (to grow up).

**But when you use words like these, it shows you're not praying for people? Just pray for them, and that's it.**

These are God's words, not ours. These scriptures were all written by men of God filled with the Holy Ghost. Did Jesus Christ not pray for anyone? He called Peter Satan, and still prayed for him. Did Paul, Jeremiah, Isaiah, Samuel, Nehemiah, and Nathan all refuse to pray for anyone? Teaching and Preaching these words AND praying for others is the way to do God's work.

> *1 Samuel 12:23 Moreover as for me, God forbid that I should sin against the Lord in **ceasing to pray for you**: but **I will teach you the good and the right** way*

Obviously prayer and teaching are connected. It's the prayer that helps you teach people the good and the right way.

### Replacement Referees Can't Call It

There was a recent period in the National Football League where they had replacement referees because the real referees were locked out. People were complaining, making jokes about all the obvious bad calls that were made in the games where replacement referees were in charge.

Late night talk shows started clowning and cracking on replacement refs, and the ridiculous calls they were making. Twitter was full of jokes about replacement refs. If we took the Kingdom of God as seriously as we did football, maybe we would protest the bad calls that go on in the church that bring shame to the name of God?

Maybe God can show us from the football situation how the church looks when we put baby Christians in charge that can't discern between good & evil... There's replacement refs all over the church right now!

> *Hebrews 5:13*
> *For every one that useth milk is unskillful in*
> *the word of righteousness: for he is a babe.*
> *But strong meat belongeth to them that are of*
> *full age, even those who*
> *by reason of use havetheir **senses exercised to discern b***
> ***oth good and evil.***

**We Have to Protest.** If people can complain about bad calls in a fun but vain game that is filled with alcoholism, physical lust, and excess. How much more should we be protesting bad calls in the Church, where eternal souls are in the balance?

When someone can switch from the broad road to the narrow road, and keep 95% of their followers in the Church, there are a lot of replacement refs not making the right call, and people are headed to destruction because of it.

There are 2 types of replacement refs in the church – babies and wolves. Babies are immature, but when they get corrected, they change. They repent with real fruit. Plus they start making the right call.

Wolves are there to steal and spiritually consume Gods sheep. They are the thieves in the house of prayer, like Tobias in Nehemiah. As I've mentioned before, Tobias opposed the building of the walls of Jerusalem (symbolizing protection, holiness, and separation), but then got himself a room in the temple because he did so much business with the elders of Jerusalem. The Levites were kicked out and had to go work the fields.

In the book of Nehemiah, the elders of Jerusalem would be the spiritual babies. Tobias would be the wolf. Nehemiah is the real ref, who rebukes the elders of Jerusalem, kicks Tobias out, and puts the Levites back in their place.

### How Can You Tell the Difference Between Spiritual Babies and Wolves?

When spiritual babies get corrected, they repent, and bring the fruits of repentance, and grow into mature sons of God. Spiritual maturity is not based on age or time, it's based on obedience.

When wolves are corrected or instructed of error, wolves don't repent. They may not even let you correct or communicate with them. They may just duck & hide and bite and never even admit they did anything wrong. Wolves just kill, eat, and move on. They are ravenously hungry wolves (Matthew 7).

Whether you are protesting the baby Christian, or the wolf, just make sure things are changed. It's not about who they are, **it's about what they're doing.** You can't judge them, **you can only judge their fruit.**

Yes you have to confront people, but the main thing is to **point the finger at the Word of God.**

People can always make an excuse, and say: "Every time you point the finger at someone else, 4 other fingers are pointing back at you."

I prefer to say this: "Every Time I Point A Finger at the Word of God, 9 other fingers point back at me, telling me I should keep following the Word of God instead of the lies of men."

But what if they call me a Pharisee? Here are some tools:

### BIBLICAL TOOLS so that you can Teach and Discern Holiness versus Hypocrisy and "Pharisees"

### The leaven of the Pharisees is NOT Holiness.

### What is holiness?
Holiness is beautiful to God. Holiness is separation to his purpose and unto him alone. It's sanctification. It helps start the dawning of a new powerful day in God's Kingdom. Holiness is especially beautiful among youth.

> *Psalms 110:³ Thy people shall be willing in the day of thy power, in the **beauties of holiness** from the **womb of the morning**: thou **hast the dew of thy youth**.*

## The Leaven of the Pharisees is Hypocrisy and Covetousness

Pharisees are actors in real life who are excellent at making money for saying the word while not doing it.

> *Luke 12:1 In the mean time, **when there were gathered together an innumerable multitude of people,** insomuch that they trode one upon another, he began to say unto **his disciples first of all, Beware ye of the leaven of the Pharisees, which is <u>hypocrisy.</u>***
>
> *² For there is nothing covered, that shall not be revealed; neither hid, that shall not be known.³ Therefore whatsoever ye have spoken in darkness shall be heard in the light; and that which ye have spoken in the ear in closets shall be proclaimed upon the housetops.*
>
> *⁴ And I say unto you my friends, Be not afraid of them that kill the body, and after that have no more that they can do.⁵ But I will forewarn you whom ye shall fear: **Fear him, which after he hath killed hath power to cast into hell**; yea, I say unto you, Fear him.*

Notice when Jesus chose to instruct HIS disciples to beware of the leaven of the Pharisees. It was when the crowd got so big that they started to trample one another.

When the crowd got big the first and most important thing on Jesus heart was that His true disciples were wary of the temptation to become an actor like the Pharisees were. When crowds get big, that's when wolves put their masks on. That's when actors start to perform for cash instead of obey God.

The Pharisees thought that since they were good actors, and respected by society, God would keep their sin secret like some type of government or corporate organization would. But Jesus said that there is nothing hidden that would not be revealed

**Pharisees are also excellent at making money by doing things that look good on the outside to man but are abomination to God**

> *Luke 16* [13] *No servant can serve two masters: for either he will hate the one, and love the other; or else he will hold to the one, and despise the other. Ye cannot serve God and mammon.*
>
> [14] *And* **the Pharisees also, <u>who were covetous</u>**, *heard all these things: and they derided him.*
>
> [15] *And he said unto them,* **Ye are they which justify yourselves before men;** *but God knoweth your hearts: for* **that which is highly esteemed among men is abomination in the sight of God**.

The Pharisees were covetous and knew how to make themselves look good to men, but the things they did were an abomination to God.

Jesus's instructions to **His** disciples regarding Pharisees was: to do exactly what they say because they are really good at saying the word. But He also said "Do NOT do what they do" because they are actors, they are faking it.

Pharisees do know certain parts of the Word; and it really does take a lot of talent, authority, and intelligence to be a really good hypocrite.

But according to Jesus Christ, the leaven of the Pharisees is hypocrisy, not holiness. Hypocrites are those who are good at saying the word but not doing it. They are talented actors.

Jesus instructs HIS disciples to do what they say (of course if they can quote a couple scriptures), but NOT do what they do. Therefore you can choose to follow the actors that know how to say all the right things while they spread corruption, OR you can follow Jesus. Pharisees are the ones who love to act the part but can't bear their cross and obey God in holiness. Pharisees are not the ones that preach repentance and live holiness.

**When you decide that you are smart enough to lead God's people by talent instead of by example, you are a hypocrite and God starts the process to make an example out of you.**

> *Matthew 23 Then spake Jesus to the multitude, and to his disciples,[2] Saying The scribes and the Pharisees sit in Moses' seat:[3] All therefore whatsoever they bid you observe, that observe and do; but **do not ye after their works: for they say, and do not.***

Jesus requires his disciples to be good at doing it not just at saying it (James 1:22).

## What is Leaven?

Leaven is the yeast that fills up the whole body like a yeast infection, or a piece of bread.

## A Little Leaven Leavens the Whole Loaf

> *Galatians 5:8-9 This persuasion cometh not of him that calleth you. A **little leaven leaveneth the whole lump.***

False teaching permeates the whole Body if it is allowed to be taught verbally or by example without correction.

> **Persuasion**:
> Transliteration: peismonē
>
> 1. persuasion 2. treacherous or deceptive persuasion

> *1 Corinthians 5:6-8 Your glorying is not good. Know ye not **that a little leaven leaveneth the whole lump**? **Purge out therefore the old leaven**, that ye may be a new lump, as ye are unleavened. For even Christ our passover is sacrificed for us: Therefore let us keep the feast, not with old leaven, neither with the leaven of malice and wickedness; but with the **unleavened bread of sincerity and truth.**

When false teaching is taught by example, such as fornication, malice, or wickedness – God has to start a whole new unleavened loaf of bread a.k.a. Body of Believers, that walk in the sincerity and truth of Christ. He can do this by purging the leaven, yeast, false teaching, false example from the Body of believers. He can also send an apostle to recreate the Body and form them into Christ.

## The Leaven of the Pharisees is Hypocrisy

Pharisees don't spread holiness or the gospel.

Pharisees spread hypocrisy and spread covetousness and the love of money

Hypocrisy and Covetousness is what they spread through the Body of Christ if you don't beware.

189

A Pharisee is not the one who advocates for holiness and separation unto Gods purpose out of Love for Him.

A Pharisee is the one who preaches Holiness and separation from the world for five years and then does the opposite.

**But didn't Jesus eat with sinners?**

Jesus ate with repenters. That's why they came to eat with Jesus because they had actually repented from the sin. The Pharisees were the ones that called them sinners because of their social status not because of their fruits.

Read Luke 19, it was the Pharisees that called Zacchaeus a sinner... but Zacchaeus was the one who gave half his net worth to the poor in repentance and faith when he saw Jesus! He was not a sinner, he was a repenter, with real fruit of repentance in faith!

**But what about Evangelism?**

Evangelism minus holiness is counterfeit evangelism.

> *Matthew 23:15 Woe unto you, scribes and Pharisees,* ***hypocrites****! for ye compass sea and land to make one proselyte, and when he is made,* ***ye make him twofold more the child of hell than yourselves****.*

You can travel all you want and spend money to reach an unbeliever, but if you are an actor, your disciples are double the child of hell than you. This is why talented actor/Pharisee based evangelism is useless.

**Does Holiness mean that you are mean and you can never associate with an unbeliever?**

No. That's ridiculous.

What it does mean is that you don't follow you their ways you don't do what they do and your ministry is set apart and separate from making covenants with unbelievers

The benefit of not being joined in partnership with unbelievers, and perfecting holiness in the fear of God, is a Father/Child relationship with God.

> *2 Corinthians 6:[14]* **Be ye not unequally yoked together with unbelievers**: *for what fellowship hath righteousness with unrighteousness? and what communion hath light with darkness?*
>
> *[15] And what concord hath Christ with Belial? or what part hath he that believeth with an infidel?*
>
> *[16] And what agreement hath the temple of God with idols? for ye are the temple of the living God; as God hath said, I will dwell in them, and walk in them; and I will be their God, and they shall be my people.*
>
> *[17]* **Wherefore come out from among them, and be ye separate, saith the Lord, and touch not the unclean thing; and <u>I will receive you.</u>**
>
> *[18]* **<u>And will be a Father unto you, and ye shall be my sons and daughters,</u>** *saith the Lord Almighty. 7 Having therefore these promises, dearly beloved,* **let us cleanse ourselves from all filthiness of the flesh and spirit, perfecting holiness in the fear of God.**

When you think of fellowship, think of two people in the same boat, going the same direction, in the same ship, in the same team. Fellows in a ship. Holiness is being in a different ship, and living like it.

Holiness is being separate unto God from unbelievers, so that you can reach God, then reach unbelievers. If you compromise God's obedience to reach unbelievers, you are a hypocrite and a Pharisee, and all your reaching people is utterly useless.

So don't let anyone call you a Pharisee for protesting corruption in the Church and calling for the beauty of holiness. Most likely, they are the Pharisees themselves. Pray for them and help to open their eyes. Join the Protest!

What is the goal of the protest? To see the Lord Jesus Christ return to a Church walking in the Beauty of Holiness without Bondage to sin and vain tradition, manifesting their identity as the Sons of God.

## The Beauty of Holiness without Bondage

The Balance of the Word of God and the Spirit of God with Eyes on Jesus Christ helps you to walk in Holiness without legalism and bondage to the precepts of men.

Jesus warned us of religious leaders who teach their principles and precepts as doctrines (Matt 15). There are many teachers who aren't filled with the Holy Ghost, so they try to force the principles of the word without the Spirit of the Word. The bible says that the letter killeth, but the Spirit gives life (2 Corinthians 3).

When you focus on the heart of God, you meditate the Word and the Spirit of God. You are not averse to the supernatural elements of the Holy Spirit – dreams, visions, tongues and interpretation of tongues, prophecy, word of wisdom, word of knowledge, healing, special faith, etc... because you know that God is pouring out His Spirit on all flesh.

However, you judge all spiritual circumstances by the Scripture.
The Scripture helps you with the Spirit, and the Spirit gives life to the Scripture so that you can walk in love with God and your neighbor.

If you don't have the Holy Spirit helping you obey scripture, all you have is dead principles, failure, and abuse.

If you don't have Revelation of the Scriptures, all you have is your ignorance and foolish disobedience, with satanic deception.

You need the fullness of both the Word of God, and the Spirit of God to walk in the Beauty of Holiness without Bondage, and the Truth will

Make you Free to Walk in the Spirit of Liberty and UNSTOPPABLE LOVE.

Clear Spiritual Vision, Effective Faith through trials, and the Pure and clean Righteousness of Jesus Christ will be in your possession if you pray for it (Revelations 3:18).

The earth is waiting for the True Sons of God to show up! They won't be making excuses and cop-outs, but they will manifest God's Judgements, Love, and Powerful Faith in the earth. Even in suffering, they will be the glorious fragrance of Christ's Victory.

> *Romans 8:4 That the righteousness of the law might be fulfilled in us, who walk not after the flesh, but after the Spirit.⁵ For they that are after the flesh do mind the things of the flesh; but they that are after the Spirit the things of the Spirit.⁶ For to be carnally minded is death; but to be spiritually minded is life and peace.*
>
> *⁷ Because the carnal mind is enmity against God: for it is not subject to the law of God, neither indeed can be.⁸ So then they that are in the flesh cannot please God.⁹ But ye are not in the flesh, but in the Spirit, if so be that the Spirit of God dwell in you. Now if any man have not the Spirit of Christ, he is none of his.*
>
> *¹⁰ And if Christ be in you, the body is dead because of sin; but the Spirit is life because of righteousness.*
>
> *¹¹ But if the Spirit of him that raised up Jesus from the dead dwell in you, he that raised up Christ from the dead shall also quicken your mortal bodies by his Spirit that dwelleth in you.¹² Therefore, brethren, we are debtors, not to the flesh, to live after the flesh.*

*<sup>13</sup> <u>For if ye live after the flesh, ye shall die: but if ye through the Spirit do mortify the deeds of the body, ye shall live.</u> <sup>14</sup> For **as many as are led by the Spirit of God, they are the sons of God.**

<sup>15</sup> For ye have not received the spirit of bondage again to fear; but ye have received the **Spirit of adoption, whereby we cry, Abba, Father.**

<sup>16</sup> The Spirit itself beareth witness with our spirit, that we are the children of God:<sup>17</sup> And if children, then heirs; heirs of God, and joint-heirs with Christ; <u>if so be that we suffer with him, that we may be also glorified together.</u>

<sup>18</sup> For I reckon that the sufferings of this present time are not worthy to be compared with the glory which shall be revealed in us.

<sup>19</sup> For **the earnest expectation of the creature waiteth for the manifestation of the sons of God**.*

## The Protest is For Heaven and God's Reward, Not for Earth and Man's Recognition

There will always be false prophets with more money and more followers. You will never beat Babylon at their own game of money and fame accumulation. Talent comes from God, so there will always be a market for talent, even talented hypocrites.

There will always be false shepherds with huge followings. There will always be more people comfortable with dead men's bones than with the voice of the Holy Spirit. There will always be people that want a watered down version of the Word; having a form of Godliness, but denying the power. You will never beat wolves at their own game of eating sheep and opening the gate for other wolves at night.

**But you can stand.** You can declare, loud, clear, accurate and sharp, you can teach continually with patience, and you can lead by example. You can raise a standard, and You can always make true disciples for Jesus Christ.

You can pray and cry aloud to God in the evening, morning, and at noon. You can purge the old leaven and form new ministries if you have God's direction. The earth itself is waiting for the real sons of God to manifest, so seek His face and go do it! There is a great reward for you, because God is a Rewarder of those that diligently seek Him (Hebrews 11:6).

## This is the Generation that Seeks His Face!

The devil wants to steal kill and destroy our generation from the inside out, but Jesus Christ has defeated Him.

This victory will start to manifest when we hold the standard and say that the corruption and mixture stops here, period. Eventually God will have a generation that seeks His face so that the King of Glory can come in. It's written in **Psalms 24** so it might as well start with us!

This victory is going to continue when we refuse to follow blind leaders who do not see what is happening spiritually in the land. There are many who corrupt the Word of God. We have to follow real kingdom generals, not brand-sensitive fundraisers that are scared of the hatred, loss, and persecution that comes when they **testify, declare, and proclaim that the worlds works are evil** (John 7:7). We have to follow leaders who sacrifice their lives for the Truth. "Men that have hazarded their lives for the name of our Lord Jesus Christ (Acts 15:26)."

## Interpretation

The Protest dream was really simple to interpret, but very encouraging. What we saw in the dream was what we experienced. Our eyes were opened to the corruption of praise in Christian entertainment. What was encouraging was that when we joined the protest, God started providing for it. It was also encouraging that "Lily" stands for purity. God gives provision and a pure spiritual identity to those who stand against spiritual corruption and mixture in His Church.

In the Monster's Ball dream, God was showing us that if we stayed faithful to the protest, and prayed for them, that some of the Christian artists that were spreading iniquity would be rescued from their darkness and become brand new. He was encouraging us to stay on the narrow road instead of follow the crowd.

He was also showing us the spiritual identity of those who use ministry to promote compromise, and the spiritual fruit they end up with: bloody violence.

A Christian that constantly listens to secular music ministry to "hone their craft" or "help their ministry" is like a soldier that constantly keeps his head next to his enemies semi-automatic rifle to see how it sounds. It's only a matter of time till your head is blown off, or you've joined the enemies camp, becoming a spiritual monster. But you'll think all the sudden you got "wiser." (Genesis 3)

Then you become part of the problem, a spiritual monster, and help everybody else get their head blown off too. Brains and blood splattered everywhere. "Oops we all just fell in sin, I don't know what happened..."

It was very encouraging to know by the Spirit that some of them would eventually repent and fall back in love with God.

In the Ducking and Hiding dream, God was also showing us the spiritual identity of those we were standing against. As we said in the first chapter: when we stood against the iniquity of secular artists Jay – Z and Beyonce', Satan influenced people the church (people who go to church but still loved the secular artists that spread iniquity) to attack us.

The Ducking and Hiding dream was the same, but in reverse. This time, we were rebuking idolatry in the Church, and God showed us which spirits in the world we were really affecting. God was showing us that false prophets inside the Church were connected spiritually with false prophets outside the Church. God was showing us that spiritually, these angels of light were still following Snoop (and whatever principality he represents), and instead of repenting, they were trying to duck our words.

But God was also showing us how powerful and effective our words were, and that we were on top. The Church has authority and is always on top, and our words always have a powerful effect – even if those with the spirit of the world try to duck and hide.

## Application

Join the Protest! **Everyone has a Right to Repent.**

Take Up Your Cross and **Follow Jesus if You Really Love Him**

Disciple the "Few" Lead them into Life. **Stay Away from Following the "Many"** on the Wide Road to Destruction

Protest **Counterfeit Evangelism**: Evangelism without Holiness is a lie, because Jezebel's children eventually get killed with death (Revelations 3).

Realize that **You Are The Only Hope** for a Spiritual Awakening to God's Holiness in Your Generation and Sphere of Influence – **Your Obedience is Critical to Save Many** and Help them See God.

Protest the **Many who Corrupt and Water Down the Word to Make it Easier to Sell** – This Destroys Eternal Fruit, and Turns the House of Prayer into a Den of Thieves.

**Rescue People From Satan's False Light** into the Light of the Word of God.

Walk in Your Authority and **Watch God turn His Enemies into His Footstool –** He uses them to Rest His Feet and Bring His Body Higher!

Everyone has a Right to Repent. Confront and **Kill Idols for Revival! If we do, We will See the Harvest and Hasten the Return of Jesus (2 Peter 3:12).**

# Appendix A

## SPIRITUALS AND NATURALS OF FASTING

### First question - Is fasting a new covenant spiritual practice?

**Answer**: Yes, now that Jesus is physically not here, his disciples who love the bridegroom will fast. Fasting doesn't change God, fasting changes Jesus Christ's disciples that do it. It makes them a new wineskin, opens their soul to believe more and receive more from God's Spirit.

> *Matthew 9:14 Then came to him the disciples of John, saying , Why do we and the Pharisees fast oft, but thy disciples fast not? 15 And Jesus said unto them, Can the children of the bridechamber mourn , as long as the bridegroom is with them? but the days will come , when the bridegroom shall be taken from them, and then shall they fast . 16 No man putteth a piece of new cloth unto an old garment, for that which is put in to fill it up taketh \*from the garment, and the rent is made worse. 17 Neither do men put new wine into old bottles: else the bottles break , and the wine runneth out ...*

### How do we fast?

**Answer**: Secretly, before God. You don't have to hide it, and it's not a sin if someone finds out that you are fasting. The main point is not to show off or make it obvious, just show it to God. Of course, corporate fasts may have to be publicly announced, since they involve a whole group of people (Joel 2).

> Matthew 6:16 Moreover when ye fast , be not, as the hypocrites, of a sad countenance: for they disfigure their faces, that they may appear unto men to fast . Verily I say unto you, They have their reward. 17 But thou, when thou fastest , anoint thine head, and wash thy face; 18 That thou appear not unto men to fast , but unto thy Father which is in secret: and thy Father, which seeth in secret, shall reward thee openly *.

## What should we fast for?

**Answers:** The first reason to fast is Bridegroom love and hunger for God (Matthew 9). The other reasons are to loose the bonds of wickedness, let the oppressed go free, to break wicked spiritual powers, to give to the hungry, to relieve spiritual and economic burdens, and to get guidance and spiritual light in your soul. We do NOT fast for arguments, strife, and debate, and to point fingers at people we don't agree with. We do NOT fast to get power to wrestle against people, but to wrestle against principalities and powers of oppression that are deceiving people and oppressing people(Ephesians 6).

> Isaiah 58:4 Behold, ye fast for strife and debate, and to smite with the fist of wickedness: ye shall not fast as ye do this day, to make your voice to be heard on high. 5 Is it such a fast that I have chosen ? a day for a man to afflict his soul? is it to bow down his head as a bulrush, and to spread sackcloth and ashes under him? wilt thou call this a fast, and an acceptable day to the LORD? 6 Is not this the fast that I have chosen ? to loose the bands of wickedness, to undo the heavy burdens, and to let the oppressed go free, and that ye break every yoke?

*7 Is it not to deal thy bread to the hungry, and that thou bring the poor that are cast out to thy house? when thou seest the naked, that thou cover him; and that thou hide not thyself from thine own flesh? 8 Then shall thy light break forth as the morning, and thine health shall spring forth speedily: and thy righteousness shall go before thee; the glory of the LORD shall be thy rereward . 9 Then shalt thou call , and the LORD shall answer ; thou shalt cry , and he shall say , Here I am. If thou take away from the midst of thee the yoke, the putting forth of the finger, and speaking vanity; 10 And if thou draw out thy soul to the hungry, and satisfy the afflicted soul; then shall thy light rise in obscurity, and thy darkness be as the noonday: 11 And the LORD shall guide thee continually, and satisfy thy soul in drought, and make fat thy bones: and thou shalt be like a watered garden, and like a spring of water, whose waters fail not.*

## What's the Best thing to Do while Fasting?

**Answer**: Sit with God, Talk to Him, Sing to Him, Read the Word, Pray for People.

## Can you fast anytime you are hungry for God, or only when you are praying all day?

**Answer:** Yes, it's true that fasting and prayer are often linked together, because that's the best thing to do while you are fasting. However, you can fast while you do other things as well. You may not be able to do a lot of physically strenuous work while you fast, because fasting decreases your energy level. But you can go to work or school and live life regularly while you fast. You can fast anytime you want to, and are hungry for God enough to do it. Don't fast for legalistic reasons - only fast if you want to. You can also fast if God is leading you to.

If you look at Matthew 6, Jesus talked about 3 things to do in secret when you are seeking the Kingdom. He talked about giving, praying, and fasting. Fasting is giving **energy** to God. Praying is giving **time** to God. Giving is giving **finances** to God. Your time, your energy, and your money are **your major resources**. Jesus put fasting on the same level as the other two – a regular part of the Kingdom lifestyle. Each one can stand alone, and they can be mixed and matched. Don't feel bondage that you can only fast if you are praying at the same time. You can fast any time you are hungrier for God than food.

**What are some different types of fasts?**

**Answer:** Here are some different fasts, some biblical, and some that I made up, in order from hardest to easiest:

**40 day water**: No food for 40 days, just water. (Moses, Jesus).

**Esther Fast**: No food No Water 3 days. This is an extreme fast because it's done with no water. Anything longer than this and you might die, so I don't suggest trying to extend this one.

**Lifestyle Fast - 3 day water**: No food for 3-21 days. These can be done once a month, to once a quarter, to once a year, depending on your schedule and your desire for God.

**Quick Fast:** No Food or Water for 24 Hours. I made this one up; it's like an Esther fast cut in 1/3rd. You can do this weekly.

**Daniel 1 Pulse Fast:** Only Eat Fruits & Nuts, Beans & Vegetables, and Water to Drink: (Only plants: no bread, or meat, or sweets). This can be as long as you want it.

**Daniel 10 No Meats No Sweets Fast:** No meats, No sweets, or pleasant bread. Regular bread is ok. This can be as long as you want it.

**Fave Media Fast**: This is a fast from your favorite source of entertainment media. Whether it be a certain website, social network, sport show, radio show. I like basketball, but once I fasted all basketball related media (websites, video games, tv) for 40 days. I still played it, but I didn't entertain myself with basketball media. It blessed my soul.

**Dragon's Flood Fast (Revelations 12:15,16):** Satan sends a flood of filth from his mouth through entertainment and media to drown God's people. The Dragon's Flood fast is removing your eyes, ears, and mind from all of the wickedness that Satan promotes through entertainment and media to drown your spirit (adultery based storylines, foul comedies, talk show hosts with poisonous attitudes, porn/lingerie/swimsuit media, secular music, secular movies). This is a fast I made up, but it's based in scripture (2 Corinthians 7:1). I know people that have done it and been delivered from demons, deception, and spiritual ignorance. This is the easiest fast, and should probably be permanent!

# Appendix B

## 3 MAIN DOCTRINES THAT JESUS HATES IN THE 7 FINAL MESSAGES TO HIS CHURCH

In Revelations 2 and 3, Jesus gives 7 messages to His Church. Within those messages are 3 Main Doctrines that come up several times. They are Balaam, Nicolaitanes, and Jezebel. Jezebel is covered in Chapters 1 and 8 in this book. Let's take a look at Balaam and the Nicolaitanes.

**Jesus Hates the Doctrine of Balaam**

> *Revelations 2:14 But I have a few things against thee, because thou hast there them that hold the doctrine of* <u>*Balaam, who taught \*Balac to cast a stumblingblock*</u> *before the children of Israel,* <u>*to eat things sacrificed unto idols,*</u> *and to* <u>*commit fornication*</u>*.*

If you go to the book of Numbers and read chapters 22-25, you will see that Balaam was a prophet of God. A wicked King named Balak was scared of Israel taking over his land. So Balak promised Balaam a bunch of money and rewards to get Balaam to curse the people of God for money. Balaam could not get himself to curse the people that God had blessed. He could not prophesy falsely, or speak incorrectly with his gift. But he really wanted the rewards and money. So he came up with another strategy: He taught Balak to tempt the people of Israel with foreign women, so that they could marry them, <u>mix with them</u>, and then end up worshipping false idols.

*Numbers 31:16 Behold, these caused the children of Israel, through <u>the counsel of Balaam,</u> to commit trespass against the LORD in the matter of Peor, and there was a plague among the congregation of the LORD.*

There are people now that will say all the right things, they'll preach right, they won't deny Jesus or teach false doctrine... But they really want the money, so they will present the Body of Christ with mixture so that eventually some God's people are tricked into serving the same idols as the world. Balaam also represents someone who wants to be a bridge between the world system of Babylon and the people of God. They think they represent the best of both worlds, but that is a lie. A friend of the world's system is an enemy of God (James 4:4).

## Jesus Hates the Deeds of the Nicolaitans

*Revelations 2:6 But this thou hast , that thou <u>hatest the deeds of the Nicolaitans,</u> which I also hate .*

Nicolaitan comes from the Greek words, *nikos* meaning "conquerer" or "destroyer," and *laos*, meaning "people." Nicolaitans have the mentality of "conquering the people." It is a dividing and conquering of clergy and laity, instead of Jesus's leadership style, which is serving the people, training the people, and sending the people, in the context of humble relationships as brethren.

*Matthew 23:8 But **be not ye called Rabbi:** for one is your Master, even Christ; and all ye are brethren. 9 And **call no man your father upon the earth:** for one is your Father, which is in heaven. 10 **Neither be ye called masters:** for one is your Master, even Christ. 11 But he that is greatest among you shall be your servant. 12 And whosoever shall exalt himself shall be abased ; and he that shall humble himself shall be exalted*

Jesus taught that instead of creating religious systems where we lord over each other with titles and spiritual fatherhood, we should instead seek humility and servant-hood under God our Father in Heaven and Christ our Master. Contrast that with Diotrephes, who loves to have the pre-eminence.

> *3 John 1:9 I wrote unto the church: but Diotrephes, who loveth to have the preeminence among them, receiveth us not.*

**Pre-eminence:**
1. first in time or place ,in any succession of things or persons, first in rank
2. influence, honour
3. chief
4. principal
5. first, at the first

Loving the pre-eminence causes you not to receive Godly messengers and choose not to receive Godly brothers. It causes you to make false accusations against people and not be satisfied unless you are on top.

Of course, there are biblical instances where, for a season, an older believer sows the Word and sows their life into a younger believer. They set an example for them in servant-hood. This is an example of a Godly relationship, not an authoritarian religious construct that Jesus was prohibiting by teaching doctrines on servant-hood and His hating the deeds of the Nicolaitans.

**Summary of 3 Main Doctrines that Jesus Hates**

1. Doctrine of Balaam: Set Stumbling Blocks before God's people so they can:

> A. Eat food (harmless substance) that has been sacrificed to false gods.

> B. Commit Fornication (spiritual and physical)

2. Doctrine of Nicolaitanes: Conquering & Corrupting God's people so they can:

> A. Commit Fornication (spiritual, physical).

> B. Eat food (harmless substance) that has been sacrificed to false gods.

> C. Nicolaitanes is linked closely with doctrine of Balaam. Nicolaitanes means " to conquer laity."

3. Doctrine of Jezebel: False Prophetess, False Teaching, Seduces Gods people to:

> A. Commit Fornication (spiritual, physical).

> B. Eat food (harmless substance) that has been sacrificed to false gods.

Notice that all of these doctrines that Jesus HATES have the same goal, but accomplish it different ways.

Balaam uses trickery. "Just try it this way, it's okay."

Nicolaitanes are forceful. "Do it! You're ___ if you don't. It's okay."

Jezebel uses seduction and teaching by example. "It'll be alright, it feels good... it's okay." "You'll reach more people." "Look at me, don't you want what I have? Well, do what I do."

**Fornication**: Sexual pleasure & contact outside of marriage. Sexual pleasure is derived from chemicals that flow through your brain and bloodstream. It can be stimulated by sight, touch, and other senses. It is derived from your mind, and therefore, your mind is in control of it. Stop it. (Colossians 3:5).

Spiritually, it is allegiance to any Gods other than the true God (Isaiah 23:17, Ezekiel 16:26). It can also mean financial business agreements with sin involved.

**Eating food sacrificed to idols**. The Bible is clear that there are harmless things that would be otherwise okay, if they weren't offered up to demons (1 Cor 8, 1 Cor. 10:28). In our culture it's hard to understand this because we don't live the same way they did. In their culture, the priests of the idol "god" of the city would promote feasts, games, festivals, etc. It would be like a party or concert or festival "sponsored by Diana", or "Zeus." It was kind of like corporate sponsorship today. "The Olympics, brought to you by ACME Inc." They didn't have TV, Movies, CDs, or Radio, or Internet. Festivals like this were the main entertainment and pastime of cultures surrounding the New Testament.

Any Christian knows that a piece of chicken is just a piece of chicken. God made it, God owns it. Eat it if you're hungry! **But** all over the New Testament (Acts 15:20,29, 1 John 5:21), God instructs His people to display their love for Him by refusing to eat food that had been *openly and knowingly* offered to false gods. It's not about the food, it's about your **love for your true God** and **love for your neighbor** in not to causing them to stumble by seeing and following your example.

Although health is an entirely different subject, there are really no "demonic chicken dinners" or "idolatry pizza parlors" around anymore. Nowadays, the idols of entertainment take **harmless music**, and lace it with **demonic deception – lyrically**. They take harmless **movies**, and sacrifice them – **via the script** to the false gods of greed, fornication, false religions, relativism, atheism, violence, theft, homosexuality, etc.

Beware of those doctrines that Jesus HATES! They will try anyway they can to get you to accept fornication, idolatry, and compromise:

**Balaamites** will trick you into compromise.

**Nicolaitanes** will force and corrupt you into compromise.

**Jezebellians** will teach and seduce you into enjoying compromise.

Stick with Jesus, your first love!

# Appendix C

## SUMMARY OF PRINCIPALITIES AND STRONGHOLDS THAT WILL BOW TO JESUS

### Summary of Principalities and Strongholds that will Bow to Jesus in Detroit

This is a summary of the revelations of Principalities and Strongholds in Detroit that God has given me and my wife through dreams, interpretations, our testimony, and the Word of God.

Our basic premise is Matthew 16 and Matthew 18. The Church already has All the Authority. "If it's bound, the Church bound it. If it's loosed, the Church loosed it." When our obedience is fulfilled, God can revenge all disobedience (2 Corinthians 10). Therefore, we must repent and allow God's word to change our minds if we want to see change, because it's mostly our fault (Daniel 9). We must repent from:

1. **Tolerating Jezebel**– Toleration of Compromise, Spiritual Fornication, Teaching Idolatry
    1. Music and Ministry that mixes, and partners with the World (fornication). Christian musicians and singers and preachers that partner with the world usually end up in spiritual or natural fornication or adultery, or divorced. The natural is just a reflection of what they've already done spiritually.
    2. Music and Ministry that copies and follows the World (teaching God's servants to eat food that has been sacrificed to idols). The best way to teach is by example. If our "top" singers, rappers, and musicians copy and remix and partner with the world, they pollute the whole church.

3. Detroit has been the prototype city for allowing our Levitical sons and daughters to be seduced by Jezebel instead of giving God pure worship. From mammon and politically compromising preachers to our compromising singers, we let God's priests and Levites make music about money and adultery instead of worshipping Him.
4. There is a famous Detroit pastor who sang, sold his sermons, charged exorbitant fees to speak, had several adulteries, broken marriages (apostasy is divorce), and had a baby by a 13 year old in his own congregation. He encouraged his daughter to mix with the world and sing soul music for money. All this was done in the 1930s and 1940s, and we tolerated it – even celebrated this. Now we have generations that worship talent instead of God, so they are easily deceived.
5. Afterwards, Motown became the prototype record label to all the labels that exist now. Their first hit song was "Money, That's what I want." Their second was "Gotta Shop Around." Idolatry and Adultery. Most of their musicians and singers were children from the Church. Even the Beatles first hit song was a Motown song (Money, That's What I Want). The negative and positive influence of Detroit on the world is mind-boggling.
6. Even some of our gospel music copies and steals from the world – rejecting God's creativity. We think it reaches more people, but according to Jesus – Jezebel's doctrine is the depths of satan.
7. There are serious repercussions to tolerating Jezebel, some of the most serious repercussions in the 7 letters to the Churches Revelations 2-3.
8. Lustful looks among men, Sexual Dress among women

2. **Judas's Pragmatism**– Betraying the Will and Purpose of God by following our own Mind and doing "What Works"

1. The Detroit region is a stronghold for pragmatism. The industrial mentality can become "pragmatic" which is an extreme version of practicality. Henry Ford was known to be very practical, and influenced by pragmatism. Obviously, practical thinking can be used for good. However, pragmatism as a philosophy can be very evil. Henry Ford was known to be anti-Semitic. We do not know if his pragmatic way of thinking was the cause of his anti-Semitism.

2. "Enemies of the cross, mind earthly things" – Philippians 2. Practical thinking that is not rooted in obedience to God's will is pragmatism and self-worshipping disobedience. Earthly mindedness leads to satan entering in your mind. Jesus called both Judas and Peter satan when they exhibited earthly mindedness.

3. Judas was earthly minded. God got His will done anyway, but "woe to him that betrays the Son of man." We betray the purpose of our single lives, our families, our ministries, our churches when we put our will to do what we think will work above the scripturally stated will of God for each ministry.

4. We Are Responsible for Abortion (The Judas Kiss). Racist eugenicist Margaret Sanger got family planning and birth control accepted in the church for "pragmatic" reasons nearly 40 years before abortion was legalized. She had genocide in her philosophies, but she didn't say it outright. In the name of women's health, contraception, and family limitation, she convinced us that children were a loss, not a profit; we should limit our families to what we think we can afford pragmatically. Her motto in her publication – Woman Rebel was "No Gods, No Masters." We let her in the church and loosed it with our own authority.

5. Contrary to popular belief, Margaret Sanger was NOT pro-abortion, she was against abortion, and she promoted birth control and family limitation because she thought it was best for woman. She was funded by racists who wanted to destroy the Negro race by limiting their population growth. The anointing of

motherhood is the only thing that stops the spirit of abortion which comes from family limitation. The root of abortion is not a law, it's a mindset of pragmatism related to family planning and racism.

6. Some of us lose the anointing for increase because we purposefully limit God's increase of godly seed. Earthly mindedness makes us think backwards. Purpose creates income, income doesn't create purpose.

7. We can't point at Democrats to blame for abortion, or Republicans to end abortion when we have all the authority. We are above them. Get birth control and family planning out of the Church and abortion falls in the government, guaranteed.

3. **Dog-tongues and Wolfpacks**– Using Our tongues against our brothers, Ministries whose purpose is to tear down and steal from other ministries

1. Using our tongues like dogs. Speaking negatively about other people, other ministries, other races, other churches.

2. In many churches, every sermon has a "diss" of someone elses ministry in it. "That big church" "That small church" "That Baptist dollar" "Those Holy rollers". "White people"

3. We have authority over the atmosphere in our city... so Why is our city so violent? How is gang warfare any different from using our tongues against other churches? Our mouths and especially our pulpits create atmosphere.

4. Destroying Dog-tongues and Wolfpacks. We need to create a culture of thanksgiving, blessing, honor, and intercession for people made in the image of God.

4. **Dead Men's Bones and Hypocrites**– Worshipping Traditions and Dead Men instead of following the Holy Ghost

1. Resisting the Holy Ghost instead of at least supporting the new things that God Sovereignly does in each generation. Traditions make the Word of God void of power. In the past Detroit has been one of the most tradition – loving cities.

2. We need to honor the old, and support the new. Both the New Wine and the Old wine can be preserved.

3. Return the hearts of the Fathers to the Children, and the Hearts of the Children to the Fathers.

4. Dead Men's Bones and Hypocrites – It affects the legacy of the next generation. We destroy our children spiritually when we don't allow them to create new wineskins for God's new wine to flow in.

5. **Division and Thieves**: racial division and denominational division, not being a house of prayer for all nations.

   1. We need to stop being the world's best example of racial division on every Sunday. It's loosed in the world because it's loosed in the Church. We need desegregation in the Church.

   2. Being a place where thieves can hide, instead of a house of prayer for every ethnic group. Our di-vision makes our vision smaller, and therefore we don't feel the need to pray night and day for all nations.

   3. This is also related to Judas and Jezebel, because it has to do with the purpose of God for the Church, and also the Music Ministry. If thieves steal the house of prayer from the Church, it's a den of thieves. If Levites can't or won't be employed to worship God day & night, Jezebel and Judas have victory over them and steals their calling.

   4. Real Unity – One Mind on Jesus and Mouth on Christ.

   5. The House of Prayer for every nation requires unity, regionally and racially.

   6. A House of Prayer for Every Ethnos.

   7. Dividing ourselves from each other instead of finding agreement in our different roles.

6. **Babylon Business Principles in the Kingdom of God**: brand warfare, usury, false balances, manipulation, slavery, witchcraft (pharmakia)

   1. Building our brands over being concerned with people.

   2. Putting profit before truth.

   3. Defrauding each other to the point where we need lawyers to judge.

   4. Embracing usury and debt, enslaving Gods' people.

   5. Not keeping communication and transactions in simplicity (Romans 12).

6. The Fear of the Lord is the Key to Economic Development.
7. Spiritual Sharecropping. I included this because I heard a presentation – on how Industrial Sharecropping (keeping races separated geographically, artificially manipulating the business tax base, and cost of living) effectually continued some of the basic tenets of slavery in Detroit until the 1980s – that enlightened me to the possibility of spiritual sharecropping.
8. The church has all authority, so if it's loosed, it's because we loosed it. If slavery lasted until the 1980's here, then the Church here was responsible. Perhaps the doctrine of the Nicolaitans is the culprit. We may need repentance in some of these areas or in our business principles.

Where Sin Did Abound, May Grace Much More Abound! We believe that when these false heads and spiritual strongholds are repented of, chopped off, and destroyed, The Body will be able to put our full focus on Jesus Christ, the Beautiful One.

# Appendix D

# 5 LEVELS OF CONFLICT YOU DEAL WITH IN YOUR LIFE

## 1 – Glory Overlooks a Transgression

*Proverbs 19:11 The discretion of a man deferreth his anger; and it is his glory to pass over a transgression.*

*1 Peter 4: 8 And above all things have fervent charity among yourselves: for charity [love] shall cover the multitude of sins. 9 Use hospitality one to another *without grudging.*

*Proverbs 10:12 Hatred stirreth up strifes: but love covereth all sins.*

*Matthew 5: 43 Ye have heard that it hath been said , Thou shalt love thy neighbour, and hate thine enemy. 44 But I say unto you, Love your enemies, bless them that curse you, do good to them that hate you, and pray for them which despitefully use you, and persecute you; 45 That ye may be the children of your Father which is in heaven: for he maketh his sun to rise on the evil and on the good, and sendeth rain on the just and on the unjust. 46 For if ye love them which love you, what reward have ye ? do not even the publicans the same?*

Many transgressions, sins, and conflicts can be overlooked. You can do this especially when you are rich in the Kingdom and filled with love and the glory of God. Sometimes you literally forget, or don't even notice negative things that happen to you.

### 2 – Communicate Trespasses that You Can't Forget

> ***Matthew 18:15*** *Moreover if thy brother shall trespass against thee, go and tell him his fault between thee and him alone: if he shall hear thee, thou hast gained thy brother.* ***16*** *But if he will not hear thee, then take with thee one or two more, that in the mouth of two or three witnesses every word may be established .* ***17*** *And if he shall neglect to hear them, tell it unto the church: but \*if he neglect to hear the church, let him be unto thee as an heathen man and a publican.*

There are some things that you can't forget when you try to "overlook it." Instead of letting those things, fester, communicate the problem. Matthew 18 gives a three step process.

1. Communicate with that person.
2. Communicate with them and one or two or more people
3. Communicate the problem to the Church.

If there is no repentance, just forgive and separate, agree to disagree. Always forgive the person and let it go, so that God will forgive you.

> ***Matthew 6:15*** *But if **ye** <u>forgive not men</u> their trespasses, **neither** <u>will</u> **<u>your Father forgive</u>** your trespasses.*

## 3 - Civil or Criminal Offenses – Let The Church Judge, or Let the State Judge

a.   Civil Offenses with Believers – Let the Church Judge

> *1 Corinthians 6:1 Dare any of you, having a matter against another, go to law before the unjust, and not before the saints? 2 Do ye not know that the saints shall judge the world? and if the world shall be judged by you, are ye unworthy to judge the smallest matters? 3 Know ye not that we shall judge angels? how much more things that pertain to this life? 4 If then ye have judgments of things pertaining to this life, set them to judge who are least esteemed in the church. 5 I speak to your shame \*. Is it so, that there is not a wise man among you? no, not one that shall be able to judge between \*his brethren? 6 But brother goeth to law with brother, and that before the unbelievers. 7 Now therefore there is utterly a fault among you, because ye go to law one with another. Why do ye not rather take wrong ? why do ye not rather suffer yourselves to be defrauded ? 8 Nay, ye do wrong , and defraud , and that your brethren. 9 Know ye not that the unrighteous shall not inherit the kingdom of God?*

Have the Church judge civil offenses with believers. It's better to just let yourself be taken advantage of than to sue a fellow believer in State law for a civil offense. But those believers that defraud others will not inherit the Kingdom of God.

b.   Criminal Offenses or Civil Offenses with Unbelievers – Take to Police or State Judge

When someone affects your family in a  criminal way, you can't try to overlook it, you have to protect your family. The State is God's minister to keep law and order in the land.

> *Romans 13: 4 For he is the minister of God to thee for good. But if thou do that which is evil, be afraid ; for he beareth not the sword in vain: for he is the minister of God, a revenger to execute wrath upon him that doeth evil. 5 Wherefore ye must needs be subject , not only for wrath, but also for conscience sake. 6 For for this cause pay ye tribute also: for they are God's ministers, attending continually upon this very thing.*

Civil Offenses with unbelievers can also be handled with police or with a lawyer.

### 4 – The Devil Uses People Against You, The Devil Attacks Your Mind – Forgive the People, Resist the Devil

Sometimes you will notice a higher level of conflict in your life. It may be a **pattern of trouble or conflict that goes beyond what is normal**. It could be when people that don't even know each other do similar things against you. It could be someone or several people taking the nature of satan, and being an "**Accuser** of the brethren", accusing you falsely. God may reveal something to you thru a prophetic word or a dream. This is when you need to realize that this conflict is a higher level of attack. (See Job, Joseph, Jesus, David.)

1. Forgive the people, and pray that God would forgive them for their ignorance.

> *Luke 23:34 Then said Jesus, Father, forgive them; for they know not what they do . And they parted his raiment, and cast lots.*

2. Put yourself in God's Hands with Humility and Prayer, and Resist the Devil. Don't let the Accuser Accuse Your Mind.

> *1 Peter 5:6 Humble yourselves therefore under the mighty hand of God, that he may exalt you in due*

*time: **7** Casting all your care upon him; for he careth for you. **8** Be sober , be vigilant ; because your adversary the devil, as a roaring lion, walketh about , seeking whom he may devour : **9** Whom resist stedfast in the faith, knowing that the same afflictions are accomplished in your brethren that are in the world.*

3. Condemn your real Accuser and the tongues that he uses against you.

*__Isaiah 54:17__ No weapon that is formed against thee shall prosper ; and every tongue that shall rise against thee in judgment thou shalt condemn . This is the heritage of the servants of the LORD, and their righteousness is of me, saith the LORD.*

4. Overcome the Accuser With the Blood of Jesus, the Word of your testimony in your mouth, get rid of the fear of death to walk in full obedience.

*__Revelations 12:10__ And I heard a loud voice saying in heaven, Now is come salvation, and strength, and the kingdom of our God, and the power of his Christ: for the accuser of our brethren is cast down , which accused them before our God day and night. 11 And they overcame him by **the** blood **of the** Lamb, and by **the** word **of** their testimony; and **they** loved not their lives unto **the** death.*

### 5 – Suffer Willingly from the Hand of God

The Greatest level of conflict is the suffering that comes from God. Redemptive Suffering, it's like Jesus Christ on the Cross. You are suffering for a higher purpose, to set others free. Judgment always starts with the house of God (1 Peter 4:17). Those closest to Him will often suffer first.

1. When you are Suffering at the Hand of God commit your soul to God in faith that He is doing something good for you.

> *1 Peter 4:19 Wherefore \*let them that <u>suffer</u> <u>according to the will of God</u> commit the <u>keeping of</u> <u>their souls to him in well doing,</u> as unto a faithful Creator.*

2. Know that You will always Reign after you Suffer, and be ready to receive the good results of your suffering.

> *Isaiah 53:10 Yet <u>it pleased the LORD to bruise him; he</u> <u>hath put him to grief</u>...11 <u>He shall see of the travail of</u> <u>his soul, and shall be satisfied</u> : by his knowledge shall my righteous servant justify many; for he shall bear their iniquities. 12 Therefore will <u>I divide him a portion</u> <u>with the great, and he shall divide the spoil with the</u> <u>strong;</u> because he hath poured out his soul unto death: and he was numbered with the transgressors ; and <u>he</u> <u>bare the sin of many, and made intercession for the</u> <u>transgressors</u> .*
>
> *2 Timothy 2:12 If we suffer , <u>we shall also reign with</u> <u>him</u>: if we deny him, he also will deny us.*
>
> *Genesis 45:8 So now <u>it was not you that sent me</u> <u>hither, **but God:** and <u>he hath made me a **father** to</u> <u>Pharaoh, and **lord** of all his house, **and a ruler**</u> <u>throughout all the land of Egypt.</u>*

Expect to Reign with Jesus After You Suffer with Jesus, and Keep Your Eyes on Jesus!

# Appendix E

# THE DIRECTOR'S FINAL SCENE DREAM

**Shereena's Dream**

**The Director's Chair: November 2011**

*I dreamed that Esosa and I brought an artist out to minister, but we were not having a concert. However, we were treating him as if we were doing a concert with him by being very hospitable. He was just hanging out with us at our house, I was ironing two shirts for him while he was in the back room with our children. He was very focused on the children. He wasn't just playing with them, he was hovering over them, pouring himself into them, he was focused on nothing else. My niece and nephew were with us, and the artist walked into the front room with our son Champion in his arms. I handed him the shirts, he took them but never took his eyes off of Champion.*

*Then we all started getting ready for a movie we were going to be in. My mom had been in another country but came back for the movie. It was as if all Christians had to be in this movie. The director had been ready to do the movie for a while, but he was patiently waiting for all of us to get ready. So He went around telling all of us that we had to get in high gear, because the time for waiting was over and it was time to shoot the movie. So we all started solely focusing on getting ready, got it together and went to the movie set. Everyone in the movie was part of both the cast and the crew. The director was sitting in the director's chair, he was wearing a white button front shirt with some black print on it, he had thick rimmed eye glasses and dark curly hair. He was sitting in the director's chair about to cast the vision for His movie, and we were all gathered and listening. However, the assistant to the make-up artist was not ready, she did not have her make-up on. She had covered her face with blue paste as the base for her make-up, but went out of the room to put on the rest of her make-up. She had a bad attitude and I remember thinking that I should have been the make-up assistant instead of her. I could have done the make-up but I didn't pursue it because I had so many other things to do. As soon as she left out the Director started casting the vision and the taping of the movie began. As He began casting the vision the heaven's opened and all of a sudden the earthly realm and terrestrial realm were combined and hundreds or thousands of terrestrial beings were flying around. The terrestrial realm was so amazing! The sky was dark like outer space, but there were many lights and colors in the sky that I had never seen before. The terrestrial beings were creatures but they had so many mechanical parts, they made motor sounds as they flew. I just kept thinking that I had never seen anything like it!*

## Interpretation & Application

I believe the first scene of the dream represents ministries "Turning the Hearts of the Fathers to the Children." (Malachi 4:6) Then the hearts of the Children will be turned to the fathers. God said that He would send the Spirit of Elijah to do this before the Great and Terrible day of the Lord (Malachi 4:5). Let's Do it!

Fittingly, the next scene represents the last days scenario. This is where Jesus, the Director, needs all of His people ready to participate in His last day's movie that He is directing. The one with the bad attitude was not prepared and not ready (Matthew 24). But Jesus The Director had to get on with it anyway. That the heavens opened when the Director began casting the vision shows how supernatural the last days are going to be, when there will be many supernatural signs in the heavens, and supernatural beings converging on earth, culminating in heaven coming to earth as the New Jerusalem (Revelations 3 - 21). God's People are participating in the Final Scene of the Age!

## Come Quickly Lord Jesus!

# Appendix F

# REAL REPENTANCE HAS FRUIT

*Matthew 3: [7] But when he saw many of the Pharisees and Sadducees come to his baptism, he said unto them, O generation of vipers, who hath warned you to flee from the wrath to come?*

*[8] Bring forth therefore fruits meet for repentance:*

If we want to save our churches and our families from corruption, we can't just repent from sin anymore. We have to repent from the iniquity that caused the sin. We can no longer address the outer symptoms and ignore the invisible virus, especially when God sends messengers with a prophetic microscope to make the virus visible.

*Daniel 4:27 Wherefore, O king, let my counsel be acceptable unto thee, and **break off thy sins by righteousness,** and thine **iniquities by shewing mercy to the poor**; if it may be a lengthening of thy tranquillity.*

But what about the Blood of Jesus? I thought only the Blood can wash away our sins? If we just sing a song about the blood, we'll be alright, right?

NO. Yes, faith in the Blood works, but real faith has evidence, and real repentance has fruit. Faith in the blood of Jesus brings action that is the fruit of repentance.

> James 2: [17] *Even so **faith, if it hath not works, is dead, being alone.** [18] Yea, a man may say, Thou hast faith, and I have works: shew me thy faith without thy works, and I will shew thee my faith by my works.*

## Zacchaeus Gives Us an New Testament Example of Real Repentance and Faith when He sees Jesus Christ

> Luke 19:[2] *And, behold, there was a man named Zacchaeus, which was the chief among the publicans, and he was rich.*
>
> [3] *And he **sought to see Jesus who he was**; and could not for the press, because he was little of stature.*
>
> [4] *And he **ran** before, and **climbed** up into a sycomore tree to see him: for he was to pass that way.*
>
> [5] *And when Jesus came to the place, he looked up, and saw him, and said unto him, Zacchaeus, make haste, and come down; for today I must abide at thy house.*
>
> [6] *And he made haste, and came down, and received him joyfully.*
>
> [7] *And when they saw it, they all murmured, saying, That **he was gone to be guest with a man that is a sinner.***

> *8 And Zacchaeus stood, and said unto the Lord:*
> *Behold, Lord, the **half of my goods I give to the poor;***
> *and **if I have taken any thing from any man by false***
> ***accusation, I restore him fourfold**.*
>
> *9 And Jesus said unto him, This day is **salvation come***
> ***to this house,** forsomuch as **he also is a son of***
> ***Abraham**.*
>
> *10 For **the Son of man is come to seek and to save***
> ***that which was lost**.*

When Zacchaeus saw Jesus for who He really was, it took humility. He was rich, but he ran and climbed. Rich people don't chase people, so this already showed the humility of his heart. Then Jesus called him to Himself and invited Himself into Zacchaeuses house.

Then Zacchaeus brought Jesus the fruits of repentance:

1. **Half of his net worth, he will give to the poor**. He was a tax collector, and tax collecting was a very shady industry. Since he was prosperous off of a wicked industry, he felt the need to repent by giving half of his net worth to the poor. The poor are the ones that feel the trickle down effect of wicked industry.
2. **PLUS anyone that he directly defrauded, he would pay them back 4 times what he defrauded them**. How do smart people steal? Legally, with government force, false accusations, and/or lawyers. Zacchaeus decided to pay back the people that he stole from with false accusations.

So, Zacchaeus brought real fruits of repentance for his participation in a wicked industry, AND for what he had done directly to defraud people.

Why would Zacchaeus go through all that trouble to do these things? Was it really that deep? Well maybe because as He was looking to see Jesus for who He really was, God showed him the true power and authority of Jesus? Maybe He saw Jesus's Kingdom, and His Holiness?

Maybe he saw Jesus's judgment coming on sin and iniquity? Maybe he saw what James saw:

> *James 5:1 Go to now, ye **rich men, weep and howl** **for your miseries that shall come upon you.**² Your riches are corrupted, and your garments are motheaten. ³ Your gold and silver is cankered; and the rust of them shall be a witness against you, and **shall** **eat your flesh as it were fire**. Ye have heaped treasure together for the last days.*

Maybe he saw the misery that was coming on him if he kept money that he earned in a wicked industry. Maybe he saw the fact that his unrighteously earned money would eat his flesh if he kept it.

Notice in verse 7 that they called him a sinner. But really he was a **repenter.** Jesus also acknowledge his repentance by calling it the faith of Abraham, and bringing salvation to his whole house. Then Jesus said this was his job, to seek and save the lost.

Part of the reason that repentance is one of the highest forms of faith is because it shows that you are living based on a completely new law from a completely new Kingdom, and that an earthly perspective doesn't matter to you at all. Zacchaeus would not have been prosecuted by earthly law, he was a part of it! He could have just been a good religious person and everything would have been smooth. He chose to repent because he wanted status in a new Kingdom, the Kingdom of Jesus.

So anytime someone says that we don't have to have real fruits of repentance, just declare sin and iniquity under the blood by faith – teach them this scripture.

Anytime someone says "Jesus ate with sinners," teach them this scripture – that they were "called" sinners because of social status, but really those that came to Jesus were "repenters."

Anytime someone says "Jesus came to seek and save the lost," show them the context of that scripture – Jesus is looking for someone with humility that will repent with real fruit because they see Him for who He really is.

## PAUL'S EXPLANATION OF THE FRUITS OF REPENTANCE

### If there is No Godly Sorrow, There is No Repentance or Salvation

> *2 Corinthians 7 [10]For godly sorrow worketh repentance to salvation not to be repented of: but the sorrow of the world worketh death. [11]For behold this selfsame thing, that ye <u>sorrowed after a godly sort</u>, what <u>carefulness</u> it wrought in you, yea, what <u>clearing of yourselves</u>, yea, what <u>indignation</u>, yea, what <u>fear</u>, yea, what <u>vehement desire</u>, yea, what <u>zeal</u>, yea, what <u>revenge</u>! In all things ye have <u>approved yourselves to be clear</u> in this matter.*

Godly sorrow is not glossing over and moving forward.

In 2 Corinthians 7, God was **speaking to Christians** about their repentance, not sinners. Let's look deeper into the description of Godly Sorrow and Repentance for Christians in the New Testament:

**Sorrow** – grief, annoyance, sadness

**Carefulness** – haste, eagerness, diligence to change and do right

**Clearing of yourselves** – reasoned statement on how and why you act

**Indignation** – irritation, vexation, anger

**Fear** – terror, dread of what is wrong

**Vehement Desire** – longing, strong need for what's right

**Zeal** – excitement, heat, fervor in spirit, pursuing, defending the truth

**Revenge** – vengeance and punishment, not against people but against deception and spiritual principalities

**Clear** – pure, venerable, respectable, clean

That's real new testament repentance that's when you have proved yourself to be **clear of a matter.** Imagine how different our churches, our cities, our nations would be if we didn't just gloss over scandals, or look the other way, or just blame the person who did it. What if everyone who had **partaken in the sins** of a leader – by voting, laying hands on, or promoting them – actually understood that **they were a partaker in his sins,** and then went through the process of Godly sorrow and repentance?

> *1 Timothy 5:²² Lay hands suddenly on no man, neither be partaker of other men's sins: keep thyself pure.*

There is no condemnation for those who are in Christ Jesus – that walk after the Spirit, not the flesh (Romans 8). Everyone has a right to repent. If we had a culture of Honor for God through the Fruits of Repentance, there still would not be any perfect people that had never sinned before. But **there would be a lot of people with strong ministries taking vengeance on the sin or iniquities that they came out of**, not keeping quiet about it out of the desire to honor men.

### Is It Time to Honor Men Before God?

> *1 Samuel 2:29 Wherefore kick ye at my sacrifice and at mine offering, which I have commanded in my habitation; and **honourest thy sons above me**, to make yourselves fat with the chiefest of all the offerings of Israel my people?30 Wherefore the LORD God of Israel saith, I said indeed that thy house, and the house of thy father, should walk before me for ever: but now the LORD saith, **Be it far from me; for them that***

*honour me I will honour , and they that despise me*
*shall be lightly esteemed .*

Real honor comes when we honor God. God will no longer honor blind leaders who cannot purge wolves from the flock, and choose to honor their sons and brothers rather than honor God and demand the fruits of repentance and purity. Eli was a blind leader that God held accountable for allowing his sons to pervert and corrupt the people of God and the offering of the Lord (2 Samuel 3-5).

When you read 2 Samuel 3 – 5, notice that the sins of the sons of Eli: corrupting the worship, misappropriating the finances, and laying with the women of the congregation – were all equal and related in the eyes of God. Natural adultery and Spiritual Adultery have always had a connection.

Eli rebuked his sons, but he could not stop them. God saw this and identified it as Eli honoring his sons above Him. God was offended at that.

## Seeking The Honor That Comes from God Only

Avoiding honor from men (John 5:41), and seeking the honor that comes from God only gets you access to the faith that sees the vision of Jesus Christ.

> *John 5:44 How can ye **believe** ,*
> *which **receive honour one***
> *of another , and **seek not the honour that***
> ***cometh from God only**?*

It's Time for a Culture that Honors God before it honors men.

# ABOUT THE AUTHORS

Esosa and Shereena have been married since 2008, they currently have one child and one in the oven and live in a suburb of Detroit, MI.

Esosa's great grandfather was a Pentecostal preacher. His grandparents were bible teachers and missionaries to urban youth from all over America. Esosa's father is an engineer and real estate manager, and his mother is a nurse, writer, and speaker. Shereena's mother has been an evangelist for over 20 years and her Grandmother was a pioneering evangelist in California. Her father is an award winning environmental activist.

_____

Follow Esosa on twitter @esosa

Follow Shereena on twitter @shereenamonique

Subscribe to Esosa and Shereena's Blog: www.sospression.com

Follow Shereena's Blog: www.emergefashionview.com

## YOU ARE THE KEY TO GOD'S VICTORY

You are holding in your hands the testimony of one of Christ's victories over the spiritual enemies of his Kingdom. We encourage you to take these things to heart, and spread this victory to your friends, and family.

## PLEASE SHARE WITH US YOUR FEEDBACK, ISSUES, QUESTIONS, AND OPINIONS AT:

## WWW.KILLINGIDOLS.COM

We also encourage you to help build a house of prayer in your city. This is a Unified altar of 1$^{st}$ Commandment worship and intercession to show forth the glory of the only one that is worthy. Be a living stone and join others and other churches in worship and prayer consistently. When fire burns from this altar, God's power will show up to transform us and our cities.

We also encourage you to seek ways to obey the 2$^{nd}$ Commandment, loving our neighbors in the same way we love ourselves. Never forget to minister to the poor. The end of this love is to preach the gospel of Jesus' Kingdom – and teach every people group how to obey His every command. Nothing is off limits for the authority of Jesus Christ – not religion, politics, entertainment, business, family, finances, community, environment, or anything else. Jesus Christ has not called us to just make converts, but to train disciples. We are called to produce friends of God. We are His friends, if we do whatever he commands us (John 14:6).

## YOU CAN LEAD A KILLING IDOLS BIBLE STUDY IN YOUR CHURCH OR HOUSE!

# KILLING
# IDOLS FOR
# REVIVAL

A BEHIND THE SCENES LOOK AT 9 ENEMIES OF GOD'S FLAGSHIP

Esosa and Shereena Osai

**Do it and See what the Lord does with your Purity, Power, and Prayer.**

1. Have your friends read 1 chapter a week.
2. Have people bring snacks or a drink or a dish once a week.
3. Lead a study on the chapter for the week.
    a. Talk about each chapter
    b. Read Selected scriptures Out Loud.
    c. Discuss.
    d. Ask Questions.
4. Choose 5 participants and have them choose an appendix. Those you choose will lead a study for the last 5 weeks.
5. Rinse and Repeat!

**TELL US WHAT HAPPENED at www.KILLINGIDOLS.com**

### CREATION: God made it ALL GOOD!
->God created the earth and the world and humans and all that is in the earth.

->He created you to be One with Him and have a RELATIONSHIP with Him.

->Everything was perfect, good, and beautiful.

### CORRUPTION: Sin brings DEATH!
->People (specifically Adam & Eve) sinned, rebelled against God, and brought corruption and sin, and satan (an angel that rebelled against God), into the world and into their minds. Confusion and Corruption covered the earth and all the people.

->Through one man sin entered the world.

->Death, fear, envy, lust, sickness, disease, poverty, crime, genetic mistakes, and natural disasters came after sin.

### COVENANT: The Father Gave the Promises.
->God Promised that He would send a Savior to save people and take the punishment for their sins. God gave the promise of BLESSING AND SALVATION.

->This SAVIOR was spoken about from Abraham (before Islam), to Moses (the Jewish culture was designed to prepare for the Savior), all the Old Prophets (Isaiah, Daniel, Ezekiel, etc). MANY prophets spoke about Jesus BEFORE He came.

->The Jewish Religion and the 10 COMMANDMENTS were part of that covenant to help lead people into the way of God.

->If you lie, hate people, murder, lust for sex or money or things that aren't yours, steal, or don't believe God, YOU ARE A SLAVE TO SIN. You are Judged as GUILTY by God's Laws.

->You can't keep the commandments God gave to Moses, **YOU NEED A SAVIOR** to save you and give you the power. The commandments are meant to show you that YOU NEED JESUS!

### CHRIST: JESUS Delivers the Promises!
->JESUS is Judge who is Honest enough to tell you that YOU ARE GUILTY. But then HE TAKES THE PUNISHMENT FOR YOU if you ask Him to.

->Only God could destroy the power of sin by giving his life, only Man can take punishment for being wrong. Jesus is the GodMan.

->JESUS was the one that was promised, He fulfilled every prophecy. There is ONLY ONE NAME that man can be saved by! ONLY ONE GODMAN took the punishment for you.

**CROSS: The Bloody Cross was the price for YOU!**
->JESUS paid the price and took punishment for YOUR sins, with blood, by dying.
->Sin is Punishable by Death and Blood and Hell, so Jesus paid that price for you. Only God could do it because he was Uncorrupted and Valuable enough to pay for sins. (You can't pay for anything with an insufficient funds check). Only Man could do it because man Sinned. Jesus is the One and Only GODMAN.

**CONQUERING RESURRECTION: DEATH is only Temporary.**
->JESUS then RESURRECTED because of God's power.
->The same power that resurrected him from death WILL resurrect ALL people. SOME PEOPLE will resurrect and be cast into hell and damnation, SOME PEOPLE will have Eternal Life in Heaven.
->There were so many witnesses to His resurrection, that people talked about it for centuries, and still do.

**CONSUMMATION: HE IS Coming BACK for His Friends!**
->JESUS will come back in the end of this TIME PERIOD to judge the world, and start it out BRAND NEW with His CHURCH, the people that believed and obeyed Him.
->JESUS will destroy the earth, and every person that is not with him. Then He'll make it new, and run it with his people. His Friends!!!!
->This Time Period is temporary, and its soon coming to an end. Your life is SO short. Get on God's team NOW!
Do you believe and obey Jesus? Or are you still a slave to the sin and corruption and confusion?

YOU can be free from sin, fear, pride, envy, lust, poverty, sickness, and death!!!
YOU can have ETERNAL LIFE!!!
YOU can be FRIENDS with GOD through JESUS!!!
He paid the price for your sins, so Pray to Him and be Reconciled!!!

## **PRAY WITH US:**

"Father, I thank you for Creating me in Your Image. I apologize for turning on you and following my sins. I turn my heart towards you now. I thank You for sending Jesus Christ to die on the cross and take the Punishment for My Sins. JESUS is now my Absolute Lord and King. Father, I will follow You! In the Name of Jesus, Amen.